SOCRATES:
A GUIDE FOR THE PERPLEXED

Continuum *Guides for the Perplexed*

Continuum's Guides for the Perplexed are clear, concise and accessible introductions to thinkers, writers and subjects that students and readers can find especially challenging. Concentrating specifically on what it is that makes the subject difficult to grasp, these books explain and explore key themes and ideas, guiding the reader towards a thorough understanding of demanding material.

***Guides for the Perplexed* available from Continuum:**

SOCRATES:
A GUIDE FOR THE PERPLEXED

SARA AHBEL-RAPPE

continuum

Continuum International Publishing Group
The Tower Building   80 Maiden Lane
11 York Road   Suite 704
London SE1 7NX   New York, NY 10038

www.continuumbooks.com

British Library Cataloguing-in-Publication Data
A catalogue record for this book is available from the British Library.

ISBN: HB: 978-0-8264-6377-7
       PB: 978-0-8264-3325-1

Library of Congress Cataloging-in-Publication Data
Ahbel-Rappe, Sara, 1960-
Socrates: a guide for the perplexed/Sara Ahbel-Rappe.
    p. cm. – (Guides for the perplexed)
Includes bibliographical references and index.
ISBN 978-0-8264-6377-7 (hb) – ISBN 978-0-8264-3325-1 (pb)
1. Socrates. I. Title. II. Series.

B317.A39 2009
183'.2–dc22   2008047958

Typeset by Newgen Imaging Systems Pvt Ltd, Chennai, India
Printed and bound in Great Britain by CPI Antony Rowe Ltd,
Chippenham, Wiltshire

CONTENTS

ACKNOWLEDGEMENTS

The author would like to thank Sarah Campbell, editor of the Guides for the Perplexed, as well as Tom Crick for his help with the project. Thanks also to James I. Porter for his singular work on Nietzsche and Socrates. I would also like to thank my teachers in graduate school, A. A. Long, G. R. F. Ferrari and Gregory Vlastos, midwife par excellence. Thanks, as well, to all of the contributors to the Blackwell *Companion to Socrates*, whose original research has made this work possible. In addition, the author thanks her own family profoundly and apologizes for the time away from home needed to complete the book. This book is dedicated to Karin.

ABBREVIATIONS

BT	Nietzsche, F. 1999. *The Birth of Tragedy*. Cambridge Texts in the History of Philosophy. Cambridge: Cambridge University Press.
CM	Strauss, L. 1964. *The City and the Man*. Chicago, IL: University of Chicago Press.
DL	Diogenes Laertius. 1964. *Vitae philosophorvm. Recognovit breviqve adnotatione critica instrvxit H.S. Long*. Oxonii: Typographeo Clarendoniano.
DRN	Lucretius. 1992. *De rerum natura*. With an English translation by W. H. D. Rouse; revised by M. Ferguson Smith. Cambridge, MA: Harvard University Press.
LHP	Hegel, G. 1995. *Lectures on the History of Philosophy I: Greek Philosophy to Plato*. Translated by E. S. Haldane. London: Routledge and Kegan Paul.
LS	Long, A. and Sedley, D. 1987. *The Hellenistic Philosophers.* 2 vols. Cambridge: Cambridge University Press.
M	Kierkegaard, S. 1998. *The Moment and Late Writings* (*Kierkegaard's Writings*, Vol. 23). Translated by H. Hong and E. Hong. Princeton, NJ: Princeton University Press (original work published 1854–5).
Mem.	*Memorabilia*. 2003. *Mémorables/Xénophon*; texte établi par M. Bandini; traduit par L. A. Dorion. Paris: Les Belles Lettres. Budé.
Meta.	Ross, D. 1924. *Aristotle's Metaphysics. A Revised Text with Introduction and Commentary.* Oxford: Clarendon Press.
NE	Aristotle. 1999. *Nicomachean Ethics.* Translated with introduction, notes and glossary by T. Irwin. Indianapolis, IN: Hackett.
SSR	Giannantoni, G. 1990. *Socratis et socraticorum reliquiae.* 4 vols. Naples: Bibliopolis.

SVF	von Arnim, H. F. A. (ed.) 1859–1931. *Stoicorum veterum fragmenta collegit Ioannes ab Arnim.* Lipsiae, in aedibus B. G. Teubneri, 1903–24. Dubuque, IA: W. C. Brown, 1967.
TD	Cicero. 1985. *Tusculan Disputations.* Edited with translation and notes by A. E. Douglas. Warminster, UK: Aris & Phillips; Chicago, IL: Bolchazy-Carducci.

PLATO'S DIALOGUES

Alcibiades I	*First Alcibiades*
Ap.	*Apology*
Ch.	*Charmides*
Cr.	*Crito*
Eu.	*Euthyphro*
Euth.	*Euthydemus*
Gor.	*Gorgias*
Hi. Mi.	*Hippias Minor*
La.	*Laches*
Ly.	*Lysis*
Parm.	*Parmenides*
Phaed.	*Phaedo*
Phdr.	*Phaedrus*
Prot.	*Protagoras*
R	*Republic*
Symp.	*Symposium*
Th.	*Theaetetus*
Tim.	*Timaeus*

CHAPTER ONE

SOCRATES: THE MAN AND THE MYTH

OUR KNOWLEDGE OF SOCRATES

About Socrates – son of Chaeredemus, born in 469 BCE in the Deme
of Alopece and executed in 399 BCE by the Athenian democracy; hus-
band of Xanthippe; father of three sons; and associate of Plato – we
have a few facts and many reports.[1] The most substantive of these
reports consists in the entire philosophical oeuvre of Plato, who was
28 years old when Socrates died, but who was sufficiently inspired by
his encounters with Socrates to make Socrates a central figure in all
but one of his dialogues. When we study the philosophy of Socrates,
the following is the first among the few facts that we do possess: since
Socrates wrote nothing, all that we know of his philosophy is necessarily gleaned by consulting witnesses who vary in terms of their historical
reliability, philosophical acumen and possibly prejudicial dispositions.
Socrates is one of the most documented philosophers in history, but,
as in the case of Jesus, all of these documents are the creations of people who either met him or, indeed, never met him. In this chapter, we
attempt to address some versions of what has come to be known as the
problem of Socrates: to what extent can we trace the philosophy of
Socrates woven within the threads of our various sources, and to what
extent is the philosophy of Socrates an invention of those who purport
to be writing about him? Our work here will be much more philological at times than strictly philosophical, and the question 'Socrates – man
or myth?' will accompany us throughout the entire enterprise.

THE INVENTION AND REINVENTION OF SOCRATES

Studies on the philosophy of Socrates have never been more prolific
than at the present moment. Perhaps it would not be too much to say

1

that we are living in the midst of a Socratic revival that is being prop-agated at multiple levels of academic and non-academic discourse. At one end of the spectrum are the relatively new movements, Socratic classrooms, philosophical counselling and what has come to be patented under the trademark 'the Socrates café', that now prolife-rate in the coffee shops, schools and therapy offices of major cities. These approaches seek to apply popular versions of what is often called 'the Socratic method' to the ordinary challenges of life.[2] At the other end of the spectrum are a flurry of scholarly monographs pub-lished in the past 20 years that seek to reveal the doctrinal commitments of the historical Socrates, pursuing the question with a philological ardour combined with the tools of analytic philosophy.[3] In addition, there is a renewed interest in the figure of Socrates, as it emerged in the early modern period, coupled with an appreciation of how nine-teenth-century Classical philology has shaped our own reception of Socrates and has given rise to competing interpretations of the Socratic legacy. Somewhere in between the Ivy League and the coffee shop we find a whole other approach to Socrates, inspired by the German-Jewish philosophers Leo Strauss and Hannah Arendt, both of whom saw Socrates as a civic philosopher and took the historical Socrates seriously as a political thinker, possibly even considering him the first political philosopher.

THE SEARCH FOR THE 'REAL' SOCRATES

Yet, all of this activity has resulted in some intractable problems. It now seems harder than ever to demand, 'would the real Socrates please stand up.' Some scholars deny that we can know much, even anything, about the 'real' Socrates, owing to Plato's masterful appro-priation of the figure in his dialogues, while others locate the 'historical' Socrates in the early dialogues of Plato, or find important clues in writings left by other members of the Socratic circle. When we look to these sources for the philosophy of Socrates, we find a thinker whose doctrinal commitments, if indeed he can be said to have any, are everywhere plagued by contradiction. Socrates is credited with being the first thinker to articulate a philosophy of non-retaliation, with discovering the foundations of rational action, and with formu-lating a theory of civil disobedience, on the basis of the Platonic dialogues alone. If we add in the witnesses of Aristophanes, Xenophon and Aristotle, we find Socrates practising Sophistry, engaging in natural science (or not, according to Xenophon) and inventing the art of universal definition. For yet other authors, what is distinctive about Socrates are not so much his contributions to the various philosophical disciplines of ethics, logic or psychology, but rather his life itself or even his death. In this way Socrates joins the thin ranks of people like Jesus, Mohammad and Buddha, insofar as his life becomes a model for others, perhaps followers, to imitate. Indeed, it is this imitation of the Socratic life among a group of associates that spawned the *Sokratikoi Logoi*, the fourth-century BCE literary portraits of Socrates.

Gertrude Stein, on seeing Picasso's portrait of her, is said to have complained that it did not resemble her enough; Picasso replied that soon she would come to look like it. Much the same could be said about the variety of Socratic portraits that have circulated, not only in the ancient world, but, as we shall see, in the modern and post-modern worlds as well. It would seem that Socrates is a figure like no one else, but rarely resembling himself. Who was Socrates, the man whose remarkable life spawned an entirely new genre of literature, the Socratic writings, which sought to portray this inscrutable person as exemplary? And what was Socratic philosophy, which evidently was so powerful that Plato represented him in all but one of his dialogues?

THE HISTORICAL SOCRATES

In Plato's dialogue *Phaedrus*, the character Socrates compares the relative merits of spoken versus written philosophy by suggesting that 'the living, breathing, discourse of the man who knows, of which the written one can be fairly called an image' (276a9), is actually more stable, as it is 'written in the soul of the listener and can defend itself'. In contrast, the written word 'can neither defend itself nor come to its own support' (275e7).

Plato's words of caution concerning written philosophy pertain most of all to the historical Socrates, who famously left no written work; ironically, it is precisely in the writings of Plato that we most extensively encounter his putative words. Can the only Socrates we know – the Socrates represented so variously in the sources – defend or justify his monumental role in the history of philosophy? Our task in answering this question is arduous, but not impossible; we must attend to the plurality of sources for the philosophy of Socrates without thereby reducing Socrates to a complete cipher, to being merely a reflex of the thought of those who attempted to capture him in writing.

We must honour the philosophy of Socrates in its own right, attending where possible to the ways that Socrates contributed to or in some sense was the author of a philosophical tradition. At the same time, we can notice Socrates the man, or even the Socratic way of life, that engendered literary and philosophical engagement with Socrates during his life and in the direct aftermath of his death. Where then to begin our search, not only for Socrates, but for the answer to the question the nineteenth-century German theologian Schleiermacher posed in his famous lecture of 1818, 'On the worth of Socrates as a philosopher', in which he asked how it was that 'a figure who had apparently produced no philosophically interesting doctrines . . . had been generally accorded a pivotal a role in the history of philosophy' (quoted by Ausland 2006, 485)? On what does the reputation of Socrates rest, and how has his legacy proven so prolific?

THE EARLY EVIDENCE FOR SOCRATES' LIFE AND TEACHINGS: THE 'SOCRATIC CIRCLE', PLATO, XENOPHON, ARISTOPHANES AND ARISTOTLE

Since Socrates wrote nothing, it is a fair question to ask how it is that we know anything about his life or his philosophy. In what context did people first begin recording their versions of the Socratic life, or, as in Greek, the Socratic *bios*, which in fact became an entirely new genre of literature – an Athenian literary innovation that exploited various conventions, including mime, tragedy and philosophical prose?[4] These works are not entirely fictional: they must be understood as occasioned by an event or a series of events – the uniquely towering presence of Socrates' activity in late fifth-century BCE Athens. Plato was not the only author or even the first to 'imitate the life' of Socrates: there were other members of the Socratic circle, the composition of which was reported by Plato (the Socratic literature itself, now virtually all lost, is catalogued in Diogenes' *Lives of the Eminent Philosophers*). In the *Phaedo*, the dialogue in which Plato tells the story of Socrates' death in prison, we learn that Socrates died surrounded by those who presumably were his close associates – Apollodorus, Critoboulos, Hermogenes, Epigenes, Aeschines, Antisthenes, Ctesippus, Menexenus, Simmias, Cebes, Euclides and Terpsion. Crito was present, though not listed at *Phaedo* 59b–c, and two other followers, Plato and Aristippus, were absent from the company: Plato was ill and Aristippus was out of the city.

Phaedo in addition was present, as he narrates the dialogue. Thus Plato mentions sixteen members of the 'Socratic circle': of these, fully nine are known to have written Socratic literature, while others are known, from Plato's works and elsewhere, as 'imitating' Socrates; for example, in the *Symposium* we are told that Apollodorus, 'the most fanatical in his day about Socrates' (173b3–4), adopted the Socratic habit of going shoeless. This seems to have been the only thing about Socrates that Apollodorus did get right, from Plato's narrative.

Of this early work, only fragments survive;[5] given the paucity of the extant fragments, we rely instead on other, fuller treatments of Socrates and his philosophy, including the earliest literary portrait of Socrates, found in Aristophanes' *Clouds*, published in 24 BCE, and featuring Socrates, proprietor of the 'Think-o-mat' (Greek: *phrontisterion*), suspended in a basket and presented as high priest of atheists, quack scientists and scammers. We also rely on Plato's works, which were written over a long period, presumably from 399 BCE, shortly after the death of Socrates, and well into Plato's old age, when he composed the *Laws*. The Socrates who appears in a number of Platonic dialogues that are generally labelled as 'early' or 'aporetic' (i.e. ending in irresolution), or simply as 'Socratic', in what is perhaps a question-begging classificatory scheme, is sometimes identified with the historical Socrates.[6] Finally, there is an extensive body of literature in the Socratic dialogues of Xenophon (his dates are ca. 425–386 BCE): the *Recollections of Socrates*, *Symposium*, *Oeconomicus* and *Apology*. Although his writings constitute the only other fully extant portrait of Socrates from antiquity, apart from Plato's, Xenophon's work has dubious credentials: he is only a qualified associate of Socrates (he left Athens at a young age, in his early to mid-twenties, and never resided in Athens again after his departure; how much contact he could have had with Socrates is disputable). But it is the pedantic, philosophically naive tenor of Xenophon's Socrates, as contrasted Plato's, that makes it hard to reconcile these accounts, or to arrive at a clear picture of how on their basis the historical Socrates mustered such profound influence on the history of philosophy. As Schleiermacher put it in his essay:

> What can Socrates still have been, beside what Xenophon informs us about him, yet without contradicting the character-lines and practical maxims that Xenophon definitely establishes as Socratic, and what must he have been in order to have given Plato the

inducement and right to exhibit him in his dialogues as he has done? (Schleiermacher 1818, 59)

A solution to the problem that Schleiermacher posed, to what extent does Socrates deserve his reputation as the masthead of rational inquiry, came to be formulated most prominently in the work of Gregory Vlastos.[7] Vlastos posited the developmentalist thesis, according to which a number of Platonic dialogues written early in Plato's career bore the impress of the historical Socrates, whose influence over the young Plato was marked. Moreover, Vlastos combined this developmentalist reading, which explained how Plato's thought – initially reflecting Socratic philosophy – gradually matured and achieved independence, with an emphasis on Aristotelian texts that report – exceptionally – not at all on the life of Socrates, but on Socratic doctrine and – to a lesser extent – on Socratic method. Now, given that Aristotle was born in 384 BCE and Socrates died in 399 BCE, Aristotle cannot be credited as having been an eyewitness to the life of Socrates. To the extent that he relied on Plato's dialogues or perhaps on the reports of eyewitnesses now lost, he must be seen as an interpreter of Socratic philosophy and not as an independent source. We shall return to the question of Aristotle's authority in this matter later.

To recap then, we see that from the very beginning, the figure of Socrates is problematic and perplexing: since Socrates wrote nothing, our accounts of his philosophy rely on the fragmentary remains of the work of the Socratic writers, on the caricatures of a comic poet who no doubt had at least a superficial acquaintance with Socrates, and on the extensive but fundamentally conflicting reports of Xenophon and of Plato, who himself was only 28 years old at the time of Socrates' death. Though Plato and Aristotle are responsible above all for putting Socrates on the philosophical map, we ought not to assume that this project followed in a straightforward way from the content of Socratic teaching. For it is in the *Apology*, Plato's account of the speech Socrates gave in his own defence in 399 BCE, that Socrates is represented as denying that he is a teacher, that he has any wisdom, that he knows anything 'fine and worthy' and says, 'I am very conscious that I am not wise at all'(*Ap.* 21b3). Sometimes these statements are taken to form a comprehensive 'disavowal of knowledge' on the part of Socrates, and how this disavowal can function in the context of what appears to be the valorization and introduction of Socrates as a philosopher that we find in Plato's *Apology* reminds us that our initial puzzle – on what does the Socratic legacy depend? – cannot be answered by listing and ranking source materials.

SOCRATES THE PHILOSOPHER: AN EXCEPTIONAL LIFE OR AN EXCEPTIONAL TEACHER?

Instead, we must face another paradox: since Socrates explicitly denies that he is a teacher or that he has any wisdom in the sphere that matters most, in questions of the fine and noble, in short, of human decision making or ethical philosophy, there lies a difficulty in what might seem to be a very natural assumption, namely that one ought to begin the study of Socrates with an examination of Socratic tenets and philosophical doctrines. In fact, this approach was not typical of the philosophers who constitute what one recent book has called the Socratic movement.[8] In addition to any Socratic doctrine, if such there was, it was Socrates the man, or even the Socratic way of life, that engendered literary and philosophical engagement with Socrates during his life and in the direct aftermath of his death, and later, as a philosophical ideal in the Hellenistic schools.[9] For example, Nehamas (1998) emphasizes the extent to which 'the most voluble figure in the history of philosophy' is some-one 'we do not hear at all' (70) and suggests that out of the irony of Socrates, the character Plato created and to whom he gave a 'stronger foothold on reality than he gave himself', a whole tradition according to which life can be lived eventually came to grow. Indeed, Socrates was many things: sage, martyr, possibly magus or even prophet to previous centuries, yet, in contrast, Socrates' meaning as a philosopher today is measured by an almost exclusive focus on the discovery of a Socratic doctrine worthy of the man. In other words, in starting to study the legacy of Socrates, it is important to see that the exemplary status of the Socratic life and death occasions for us a growing expectation for a Socratic philosophy that can be expressed either in terms of method or in terms of ethics and psychology, or both. This tension between emphasizing the life of Socrates and the doctrinal commitments of Socrates has more or less been conceived in terms of two ways of looking at the Socratic legacy, which we might call the 'science of happiness' and the 'art of living', respectively.

Aristotle's interpretation has very little to express about the life of Socrates and its exemplary status. Instead, Aristotle explicitly attributes doctrines to Socrates: that virtue is knowledge, that wisdom is a craft whose 'product' is happiness.[10] Sometimes Plato's Socrates also says things that appear as if he is looking to discover a science or a craft of happiness. It is a bit difficult to get the nuance of what he is after in an English translation. The Greek word that Plato frequently uses in these contexts is *techne* – a word that tends to refer to practical or productive arts, as Aristotle suggests (i.e. in the *Eudemian Ethics*). For example, at *Charmides* 172a3, Socrates says that 'once error is eliminated, and precise correctness prevails, then necessarily those who are in this condition must fare well, and those who fare well are happy'. But, as we saw earlier, Socrates always denies that he has achieved an error-free life, that he has acquired this technology of happiness, and that he has anything to contribute to such a science. For all of its appeal in terms of locating a specific set of Socratic formulations and techniques that neatly map onto the history of Western philosophy, the Aristotelian interpretation of the Socratic dialogues leaves us with very little by way of understanding of two crucial features of the Socratic enterprise, so to speak. The first phenomenon, not discussed by Aristotle but consistently emphasized by other Socratic writers, is the extraordinary life of Socrates, most evident in what Socrates calls his 'service to the city' and in his care for all members of his community, citizen and non-citizen alike; the second is his association with the themes of self-knowledge, of what might be termed his radical ignorance, and of his characteristic non-conclusiveness, all of which are continually represented in Plato's portraits.

In contrast, the 'art of living' model of Socratic wisdom considers Socrates more in terms of his exemplary life and death: his courage in the face of death, both at the hour of his execution and in warfare, his indifference to material well-being, his self-control and, above all, his willingness to sacrifice his very life on behalf of his duties to his fellow men, leading them tirelessly in a search for truth. Sometimes this art of living approach is thought to be given more prominence in the so-called Socratic schools, that is in the Hellenistic traditions of Cynicism and Stoicism that are closely linked to the ethics demonstrated in Socrates' life: his self-reliance, his care for others, his outspokenness and his exhortation to virtue.[11] No doubt, even during Socrates' lifetime, those who talked to him, whether or not they were a self-styled group of 'Socratics', differed with each other over how to interpret his philosophy. In the *Phaedo* 59b–c passage already mentioned – the gathering of his friends – Plato appears to meditate on the question of which follower deserves the mantle of Socrates' succession; who has truly grasped the teachings of the master?[12] Whatever the answer to this question may be, and some have suggested that there is more than a hint of self-advertisement here on the part of Plato, Plato ends the dialogue rather with a paean to Socrates' virtue: 'Such was the death of our comrade, a man who, we would say, was of all those we have known the best, and also the wisest and most upright' (*Phaed.* 118a16 Grube). This conclusion shows us that – whatever Socrates taught, and however profound his philosophical influence on Plato may have been – his life itself was perhaps, even for Plato, his greatest teaching.

So far we have seen that we are faced with at least two principal difficulties when we try to assess the meaning of Socrates' philosophical legacy: the first is the puzzle presented by the witnesses to Socrates, who disagree with each other, especially given the absence of any primary source material; the second is the puzzle concerning the nature of Socratic teaching to begin with – is it doctrinal, aporetic, ethical, methodological or primarily exemplary? Coupled with these initial difficulties is the magnification of possible distortion from this refractory image as it is transmitted through the various generations of those who, in their turn, identified with, valorized, or even vilified the meaning of Socratic philosophy and the figure of Socrates down through the ages, to our own lifetimes.

We have already seen that the earliest report about the life of Socrates was published in 424 BCE. The *Clouds* raises awkward, if ultimately unfair, questions for its audience: could Socrates be trusted with the youth of Athens – what were the likely consequences of his teaching? The first, unpublished ending of the play evidently bode ominously for the philosopher: the citizens of Athens collectively burn the 'Think-o-mat' to the ground. But later generations either attacked or defended the Socratic persona with equal ferocity. In the conclusion to this introductory chapter, we survey some of the thinkers who have most closely aligned themselves with or found themselves catalysed by the enigma of Socrates, beginning with the Hellenistic period and ending with a glance at modern Socratics. We must also consider briefly how the literary record depicts not merely the thought of Socrates, but also the Socratic body, which given the absence of a Socratic corpus has been 'one of the most particularized bodies of antiquity'.[13]

One author[14] has used the phrase 'midwife of Platonism' as a way to describe the philosophy of Socrates, and indeed in the *Theaetetus* we see Socrates boasting, 'do you mean to say you've never heard about my being the son of a good hefty midwife, Phaenarte? . . . And haven't you ever been told that I practice the same art myself?' (*Th.* 149a1–3 Levett/Burnyeat). The suggestion, then, is that Socrates is a philosopher who delivers other philosophers and brings their wisdom to light. Perhaps he is more a figure of thinking than a stable figure of thought in his own right, one whom others use 'to think with', and not only to think with, but also to theorize what it is to think itself. If Plato is right in calling Socrates a midwife and if it is right that, in this sense, Socrates allowed Plato to bring his own philosophy to birth, then it will be difficult enough, even from the earliest Socratic dialogues, to isolate the philosophy of Socrates. How much more difficult will it be when we wander centuries away from Athens, into different epochs, different languages, to trace the philosophy of Socrates. In the *Phaedrus*, the youth Phaedrus tells Socrates, 'not only do you never travel abroad, as far as I can tell, you never even set foot beyond the city walls' (230d2–3). In what follows, we shall find Socrates at home and also seemingly enduring prison, exile and death over and over again, not only in Athens, but also to the very edges of the Western world.

THE SOCRATES OF THE HELLENISTIC WORLD

As we have seen so far, it is more accurate to consider Aristotle a Socratic interpreter than a first-generation source for the philosophy of Socrates. We have also seen a number of people inhabiting the early Socratic circle, including of course not only Plato, but also the Socratic writer Antisthenes. Now is not the time to detail the labyrinthine pathways of Socratic succession; instead, it is easier to allude to a tradition that goes back to the *Lives of the Eminent Philosophers* by Diogenes Laertius, who posits 'an unbroken chain of teachers and pupils [that] links Socrates to the earliest Stoics' (Brown 2006). In particular, Diogenes of Sinope, the founder of the 'Dogs', or Cynics, developed the Cynic way of life while under the tutelage of Antisthenes, a close associate of Socrates according to Xenophon's *Memorabilia*. Recognizably Socratic traits of Cynicism include emphasis on virtue as a training in self-mastery and the development of self-reliance, the rejection of social authority, and frank speech.

Likewise, the Stoic emphasis on virtue as the crucial determinant of a good life, on the demands and difficulties of achieving the wisdom that arrives in tandem with this virtue, all of this may be fairly easily traced back to traits that we see emerging in the earlier Classical literary portraits of Socrates. Later, members of the Roman Stoa, including Marcus Aurelius and especially the ex-slave Epictetus, took Socrates as their role model.

Another Hellenistic school whose members advanced Socrates as their intellectual ancestor were the Sceptics: Arcesilaus, head of the Platonic Academy 273–242 BCE, evidently imitated the Socratic practice of using the interlocutor's own statements in order to secure refutations of dogmatic positions. Cicero's dialogue, the *Academica*, published in 45 BCE, is again another Roman work that places Socrates at the helm of a school of thought: the Sceptics, who embraced Socrates' methods and possibly his disavowal of knowledge as the key inheritance that made philosophy still viable. Together, the Hellenistic philosophers were powerfully attracted to the figure of Socrates, so much so that the Cynics and Stoics are now often thought of as being 'Socratic schools'. To what extent did their appropriations of Socrates see into dimensions of the philosopher that in some ways were not as pronounced in the very sources transmitted to them? This is another question that every student of Socrates must be prepared to examine.

VIEWS OF SOCRATES IN MORE RECENT EUROPEAN PHILOSOPHY

Socrates' fortunes in the Renaissance continued to wax, and as French translations based on the work of the Italian Humanists brought the figure of Socrates into French culture, another Socratic revival was well on its way. Translations of Socratic lore exerted a powerful presence in the popular literature of early-modern France. The theme of Socrates' private life appears in the satiric works of Rabelais and others, where Socrates becomes, among other things, a henpecked bigamist or lecherous buffoon. The Socrates who lived in the comedies and bawdy letters as well as in narrative paintings of the seventeenth and eighteenth centuries was rather a relic of a Roman-period Socrates, forged in traditions already obsessed with the anecdotal and the biographical (Seneca, Aulus Gellius and Diogenes Laertius). It is this tradition that gives us the apparent familiarity that we enjoy today with Socrates' marital problems, even as it rehearsed what were age-old questions concerning the moral integrity of Socrates' associations with youth. The most important thinker to treat the figure of Socrates in early-modern France was the writer Montaigne (Nehamas 1998, 101–27), who mentions Socrates' name almost 60 times in his *Essays*. He also inaugurates the tradition of French *philosophes* comparing themselves with Socrates, and the identification of Socrates as a figure for Enlightenment thought, symbol of rationality and the taming of religious fanaticism. In offering the life of Socrates as a model and in hinting that he himself is a Socratic figure, Montaigne has Socrates reinvent the Socratic art of living, which, as we have seen, has its roots in antiquity, for the modern world. How far this art of living extends into the nineteenth and twentieth centuries can be seen in the treatments of Hegel, Kierkegaard, Nietzsche and others.

In Hegel's emphasis on individual subjectivity as the essence of Socrates, there are distant echoes of Montaigne's notion of Socratic self-fashioning, and it was Kierkegaard who preserved this echo when he merged Hegel's subjectivity with his own interpretation of Socrates' negative irony. Kierkegaard's master's thesis, *On the Concept of Irony with Constant Reference to Socrates*, heralds a freedom-loving Socrates who is prone to negate conventional values. Socrates' reputation as a dissembling social critic informed Kierkegaard's own role in Danish society. In some ways, Nietzsche too turns Socratic philosophy into something personal: at once his own antagonist, Nietzsche's respect for Socrates leads him to investigate the contradictions between the figure of a robust Socrates, full of life and passion, and the dreary rationalist, founder of all in Western culture that drains the vitality from life.

SOCRATES: FIGURE OF THOUGHT OR FIGURE OF THINKING?

The methodological Socrates, the ironic Socrates, how these configurations are compatible with Socrates the moral philosopher – whether functioning as a noble exemplar that teaches tranquility in the face of death, the cherishing of truth above irrational superstition or merely contempt for the unreflecting, habitual continuation of business as usual – is not difficult to see. Perhaps more difficult to add to this picture is the figure of Socrates the eccentric (Plato's word for him was *atopos*, literally 'out of place', *Phdr.* 230d1), whether we encounter him barefooted, marching through the winter snows while on campaign in Thrace (*Symp.* 219e), or newly bathed, but absorbed, perhaps, in a contemplative trance in the midst of a wealthy Athenian neighbourhood; or learning the cure for headaches from a mysterious Pythagorean initiate (*Ch.* 156).[15] It is Socrates the unique, inimitable individual who paradoxically gives rise to the various brand names associated with Socrates: the Socratic method, the Socratic elenchus, the Socratic fallacy, the Socratic movement etc. Or, rather, it might be more accurate to say that it is in these other-worldly vignettes (Alcibiades tells us that Socrates most resembles a Silenus, a lascivious semi-human creature on the outside, while his interior opens up to reveal a divinity at *Symp.* 216e)[16] that Plato wants to leave us some egress from the Socratic stereotypes he himself generates. No doubt it is this strangeness of Socrates that convinces us most of his reality. Socrates is not only a persona, a mask, but a concretely realized individual, whose physical features we seem to see before our eyes: 'his snub nose, with eyes that stick out' (*Th.* 143e9); his thick lips 'uglier than an ass's' (Xen. *Symposium* 5.7); his pot-belly (Xen. *Symposium* 2.19); and his intense gaze (*Symp.* 221b3), along with his ragged appearance, his bare feet, his lack of bathing and so on. It is as if Socrates is the only ancient philosopher whom we could, with just a little effort, perhaps smell, so detailed are the descriptions of him (McClean 2007).

In the pages that follow, we shall have the opportunity to grapple more closely with what should in all fairness be understood as the perplexity that any initial encounter with Socrates would occasion. What we have seen so far is only the Socratic persona, literally, the mask of Socrates; beneath the mask lies an enigma that haunted thinkers from Plato to Freud. How does a conversation with Socrates, than which nothing, on the surface, appears more ordinary, give rise to the complexities of interpretation, methodological innovations, self-scrutiny and self-awareness, not to mention intimations of other-worldly wisdom, that we see first in the pages of Plato and then throughout centuries, millennia even, of Socratic reflection? We should not be in despair about the proliferation of Socrates as a figure of thought, even as we need to be cautious about reducing him to what is merely a figure of thinking. By attending carefully to our sources, by studying the details of his life and life circumstances, and by looking for those clues that bear his indelible mark, we may still catch a glimpse of Socrates.

FURTHER READING

Ahbel-Rappe, S. and Kamtekar, R. (eds.) 2006. *A Companion to Socrates*. London: Blackwell. A good account of the reception of Socrates from antiquity to the present, as are the following volumes edited by Trapp.

Benson, H. (ed.) 1992. *Essays on the Philosophy of Socrates*. Oxford: Oxford University Press. A very fine collection on the philosophy of Socrates.

Trapp, M. (ed.) 2007. *Socrates from Antiquity to the Enlightenment*. London: Ashgate.

—. (ed.) 2007. *Socrates in the Nineteenth and Twentieth Centuries*. London: Ashgate.

Vander Waerdt, P. (ed.) 1994. *The Socratic Movement*. Berkeley; Los Angeles, CA: University of California Press. This is an older and very important treatment of the various representations of Socrates.

Vlastos, G. 1991. *Socrates, Ironist and Moral Philosopher*. Ithaca, NY: Cornell University Press. Crucial for understanding the development of modern Socrates studies, as is the following.

—. 1994. *Socratic Studies*. Ed. M. Burnyeat. Oxford: Oxford University Press.

CHAPTER TWO

THE LIFE AND DEATH OF SOCRATES

THE TRIAL OF SOCRATES AS REPORTED
BY PLATO AND OTHERS

In the previous chapter we focused on the exemplary status of Socrates' life. Ironically (and with Socrates, it is always a question of irony), this life was most powerfully characterized by a dramatic death. The death of Socrates no doubt gave the immediate impetus for the spate of Socratic literature that began to burgeon in the fourth century BCE. Xenophon tells us specifically that he wrote his *Apology* for the purpose of vindicating Socrates and countering the ignominy of his conviction. Plato narrates the summons (*Theaetetus*), indictment (*Euthyphro*), trial (*Apology*), imprisonment (*Crito*) and execution (*Phaedo*) of Socrates in five dialogues, all set in the spring and summer of 399 BCE, the year of Socrates' execution.[1] Through these works, we can get a clear idea of the legal process initiated against Socrates, the charges brought against him, the defence he made against the charges and the manner of his death. Not only does this narrative unfold over the course of five dialogues, but these dialogues span a wide range of Plato's writing career, from shorter Socratic dialogues to larger works that encompass metaphysics and epistemology. Whatever else we may say about the death of Socrates, it was clearly an event that never entirely left the consciousness of Plato.

In the *Theaetetus*, we gather at least one fact about the legal process itself: Socrates has been given a summons to appear before the king-archon, a legal official who presided over cases involving homicide and impiety. At the end of that dialogue (210d1–4), Socrates says: 'now I must go to the Stoa of the king-archon, for the purpose of answering the summons that Meletus has against me.' Here we learn that one Meletus has filed a written affidavit alleging criminal wrongdoing on the part of Socrates. This *graphē paranomon*, as it was called in Greek, was the first step in undertaking a prosecution before the Athenian court. Meletus, a private individual, is known to us from the *Euthyphro* 2b8 as a 'young and unknown' poet. There Socrates explains that he received the summons; legally, the next step was to attend a preliminary hearing (*anakrisis*) and enter a plea against what were evidently the formal charges:

> This indictment [*graphē*] is brought on oath by Meletus, son of Meletus, of Pithus, against Socrates, son of Sophroniscus, of Alopece: Socrates is guilty of not believing in the gods the city believes in, and of introducing other divinities [*daimonia*]; and he is guilty of corrupting the young. The penalty assessed is death. (DL 2.40.3–7)[2]

The next mention of the legal proceedings against Socrates is in the *Apology* (speaking here in terms of dramatic date, not in terms of any supposed chronological order of the dialogues). Socrates appears before a jury of 500 (empanelled through lottery from a 6,000-member Athenian volunteer jury pool) convened for the day (some time in May or June) to defend himself in what was known as an *agon timetos* – a trial with no specified legal penalty. After the determination of guilt or innocence (*Ap.* 17a–35d), the jury voted separately in the penalty phase of the trial (36b–38b), during which the prosecutor and defendant proposed penalties and the jurors were free to choose one of these or to impose one of their own. The indictment in the *Apology* reads as follows:

> That Socrates violates the law by corrupting of the youth, and not believing in the gods of the state, but other new divinities of his own. (24b–c)

After the jury votes to convict him, by a slim margin of 280 to 220 (if 30 votes had gone the other way, he would have been acquitted: *Ap.* 36a), Socrates replies that, as he is not guilty of committing any injustice, but is rather the city's devoted benefactor, he deserves a reward rather than a punishment. However, at the bidding of his friends in the audience at the trial, Socrates proposes a monetary counter-fine of 30 *minae*; as Socrates himself has assets totalling only

5 *minae*,[3] his friends will stand as surety for the fine. The jury rejects this proposal and condemns Socrates to death. We next meet Socrates in prison awaiting an execution that has been temporarily stayed for approximately one month because of the annual commemorative voyage of a ship to the Island of Delos, in honour of Theseus' rescue of the maidens and youths to be sacrificed to the Minotaur. No bloodshed could occur in Athens until the ship's return. During this time, Socrates' childhood friend Crito visits him in prison and suggests that Socrates escape – a thing easily accomplished were Crito to offer an incentive to the guard. Socrates refuses the offer on the grounds that wrongdoing in general, committing injustice, is always to be avoided: for Socrates to leave prison illegally when it had formerly been possible for him to accept voluntary exile would undermine the laws of the city. The final chapter in the story of Socrates' death, in the *Phaedo*, is set on the last day of his life. The morning begins with a visit from his wife, Xanthippe, holding their infant son. Socrates sends her away and, later, thinks tenderly of the women of the household by taking a bath to spare them the trouble of washing his corpse. Socrates passes the day conversing with his companions, though perhaps not entirely in his usual fashion, as there is more than a hint of Pythagorean doctrine in the air. At any rate, Socrates, surrounded by a group of associates, cheerfully drinks the prescribed poison (a draught of the *Conium maculatum* variety of hemlock) prepared for him by the servant of the board in charge of the prison, called the Eleven. As the executioner hands Socrates the cup, he weeps and pays homage to Socrates. We have already seen the paean Plato writes for Socrates: 'the wisest and most just'.

THE CONDEMNATION OF SOCRATES: A MISCALCULATION OR BUSINESS AS USUAL IN DEMOCRATIC ATHENS?

How are we meant to understand the events surrounding this death? One author[4] has written persuasively that Plato's perspective on the whole affair is indicated in a telling complaint that Socrates makes just after his conviction:

> If it were the law with us, as it is elsewhere, that a trial for life should not last one but many days, you would be convinced, but now it is not easy to dispel great slanders in a short time. (*Ap.* 37a7–b2)

In other words, the trial's grim outcome was caused by a combination of events gone awry; it was a hasty and precipitate affair preceded by a series of circumstances that we shall explore more thoroughly below, namely, the defeat in 403 BCE of an oligarchic junta, the Thirty (mentioned by Socrates at *Ap.* 30), and the subsequent amnesty that gave immunity to those who committed crimes during the rule of the Thirty. There was also a spate of religious fervour within the Athenian democracy of the late fifth century BCE that saw an increase in the persecution of philosophers, as well as Socrates' decades long reputation as a suspect intellectual, an eccentric who possibly heard voices or worshipped a private deity (his *daimonion*, or divine sign, *Ap.* 31d), and who, moreover, had a pernicious effect on the youth of Athens. We have seen already that Aristophanes published his *Clouds* in 424 BCE, one quarter of a century before the trial took place; by then Socrates was already 70 years old and the father of three children who ranged in age from infancy to adolescence. When the jurors, many of whom would have seen the *Clouds* performed when they were young, sat down to try a case involving this figure of caricature, Socrates' fate was not exactly sealed, but it would have required a valiant attempt to disabuse the jurors of their impressions of the old man. On the basis of the *Clouds*, and from what Socrates himself says in the *Apology*, it would have been easy enough for the jury to believe that Socrates was a natural philosopher, one who looked for the causes of things in physical processes and who accordingly denied the truth of traditional stories about the gods. Indeed Socrates alludes to the *Clouds* in his defence; when rehearsing the 'old charges' or prejudices, he says: 'Socrates is guilty of wrongdoing in that he busies himself studying things in the sky and below the earth . . . you have seen this yourself in the comedy of Aristophanes, a Socrates swinging about there, saying he was walking on air and talking a lot of other nonsense about things of which I know nothing at all' (*Ap.* 19c2–3).

THE ACCUSATION OF 'SOPHISTRY'
IN THE ATHENIAN CONTEXT

It would have been an even easier matter for the jury to assimilate Socratic philosophy to Sophistry, the art that taught specialized techniques of persuasion to those who wished to gain influence in the city. In Plato's *Apology*, Socrates repeatedly denies that he is a teacher to begin with:

> If you have heard from anyone that I undertake to teach people and charge a fee for it, then that is not true either. Yet I think it a fine thing to be able to teach people as do Gorgias of Leontini, Prodicus of Ceos and Hippias of Elis. Each of these men can go to any city and persuade the young, who can keep company with any of their own fellow citizens they want without paying, to leave the company of these, to join with themselves, pay them a fee, and be grateful to them, besides. Indeed, I learned that there is another wise man from Paros, who is visiting us, for I met a man who has spent more money on Sophists than everybody else put together, Callias, the son of Hipponicus. So I asked him – he has two sons – Callias, I said, if your sons were colts or calves we could find and engage a supervisor for them. Now since they are men, whom do you have in mind to supervise them? Who is an expert in this kind of excellence, the human and the social kind?
> Is there such a person, or not? Certainly there is, he said. Who is he?
> His name, Socrates, is Evenus, he comes from Paros and his fee is five *minae*. I thought Evenus a happy man, if he really possesses this art, and teaches for so moderate a fee. Certainly I would pride myself if I had this knowledge, but I do not have it, gentlemen. (19e–20c)

We shall return in more detail to these 'older accusers' and the assumption that Socrates is a natural philosopher, a Sophist, or both, below.

The reputation that accompanied Socrates into the courtroom, together with what was perhaps an anti-intellectual stirring in the city of Athens, lent support to the animus that Socrates himself no doubt generated in the courtroom on the day of his trial and had also accumulated in the years leading up to it. Xenophon, in his version of Socrates' *Apology*, uses the Greek word *megalegoria*, 'boasting, big talk', to characterize the speech that Socrates gives in his own defence.[5] Socrates' alternative explanation for his popularity among the youth of Athens (i.e. that he is not a physicist and does not teach rhetoric) has this quality of arrogance about it, at least on the surface.

Socrates says that his assignment from Apollo (*Ap.* 21) sent him on a search-and-destroy mission to ferret out those in high positions and to expose their ignorance concerning matters of supreme importance, the nature of virtue. Socrates recognizes, in giving this explanation, that he has brought on himself a kind of collective hatred. Fifth-century BCE Athens was to some extent still what some might call a shame culture, where worth depended very much on one's appearance and performance in public spaces: the *ekkelsia* or public assembly, the *boule* or senate house, the courthouse itself. Here one displayed the sheen of reliable reputation or, in Greek, one's *doxa*. When Socrates went about puncturing the various social roles of those held in high esteem (as he tells us, quite deliberately: I went about searching for those who had a reputation for wisdom), he knowingly violated the politeness rules of his culture. Moreover, his demeanour in court would have exacerbated, rather than alleviated, this fundamental reputation for continued breach of etiquette.

The new charges, as Socrates calls them, are contained in the indictments, and Socrates, even his most incensed listeners must agree, actually does respond to the accusation of atheism, by using a *reductio* technique on Meletus that must have reinforced the jury's prejudices: Socrates cannot very well, while believing in divinities, not believe in gods (27a). Meletus' accusation is self-contradictory. Would this refutation impress the jury, or would it offend them, since, as Socrates says: 'remember not to create a disturbance if I proceed in my usual manner' (27b3)? Socrates further uses an analogy that was bound to rankle the jurors, with their democratic belief system, when he addresses the second charge, that he corrupts the youth. How unlikely it is, Socrates says, that only one person corrupts the youth, while all of the other citizens, the assembly, the council, everyone, improves them. Surely, 'in the case both with horses and all other animals' (25b5), one person improves them, their trainer, while other people, the non-experts, have a corrupting influence.

To compare the future citizens of the Athenian democracy to herd animals in need of a trainer – surely this fell harshly on the ears of the assembled Athenians. All of this, combined with Socrates' lack of sentimentality at the trial (he veritably taunts the jurors by not bringing his little children before them to plead for their father's life), and the culminating insult that he demands a reward from the Athenians, instead of bargaining for his life with an alternative punishment (true, in the end he is willing to allow Plato and his friends to offer the relatively significant sum of 30 *minae*, but not before the damage has been done), made up the minds of any undecided jurors.

Recall that the accusation was an *agon timetos*: Socrates was expected to suggest a counter-penalty to the capital sentence. The jury overwhelmingly voted for the death penalty during the second, penalty, phase of the trial. Yet, the question remains, did most of the jury truly expect Socrates to be executed? Perhaps some thought that he would eventually choose an exile (a possibility open to him before the trial begins, and one that he rejects during the penalty phase), even one illegally procured, rather than submit to a death sentence so hastily and even stumblingly contrived. And yet, Socrates did not leave Athens; he used neither the delay in his execution nor the influence and wealth of his friends to save himself from death.

AN ENEMY OF THE STATE? SOCRATES AND THE ATHENIAN DEMOCRACY

No doubt the remarks that Plato has Socrates make concerning the general incompetence of either expert citizens to provide moral guidance for the state or the assembled citizen body to come up with collective decisions that embody wisdom resonate with the unspoken source of anger against Socrates: his association with members of an oligarchic faction in Athens that had fairly recently staged a *coup d'etat*, imposed martial law on the citizens and exiled the supporters of the democracy. All of this took place while Socrates remained at home in the city as the Thirty, the members of the junta who took control of the state, murdered their enemies, defrauded the rich and co-opted the powerless into collaboration with them. Socrates tells the story of one such outrage in the *Apology*, but makes clear that he refused, at the risk of his life, to cooperate with their predations. It is the tale of Leon of Salamis, whom the Thirty ordered Socrates along with four others to arrest and bring to them, for the purpose of putting him to death. Rather than commit this crime, Socrates, on receiving his orders from the Thirty, quietly went home.

The bloody years of 404–403 BCE, years in which the Thirty established themselves as the government of Athens, initially by executing 1,500 citizens and exiling 5,000 democratic supporters in the Piraeus, weighed heavily on the hearts of the democrats, now returned from exile. Anytus, a champion of their cause, signed the affidavit sworn by Meletus (*Ap.* 23e: 'on behalf of artisans and politicians'). What whetted his desire for revenge was not necessarily Socrates' own membership in the oligarchic faction, but his association with people directly involved in the *coup*. Charmides, Plato's uncle, was appointed by the Thirty as one of the direct administrators of the city under its control; Critias, Charmides' cousin and guardian, was known to be a leader of the Thirty. The language that Plato uses to represent Socrates' views on education, 'Callins, if your two sons were calves or colts, we would know to whom we ought to send them' (*Ap.* 20a), is ambiguous: does Socrates imply that human beings need a trainer, someone over them to act as a moral supervisor? Is this part of an anti-democratic politics that inspired – provided a pretext for, at the very least – the oligarchic revolution of 404 BCE? Plato's *Seventh Letter* tells us of a youthful Plato, promised a place in the new state order by unscrupulous relatives who no doubt wished to exploit the young man's talents, and of a sudden revulsion on the part of Plato when he observed the fundamentally criminal nature of their enterprise. In all of this, Socrates seems vaguely if not profoundly implicated.

> When I was a young man I had the same ambition as many others: I thought of entering public life as soon as I came of age. And certain happenings in public affairs favoured me, as follows. The constitution we then had, being anathema to many, was overthrown, and a new government was set up consisting of fifty-one men; two groups – one of eleven and another of ten – to police the market-place and perform other necessary duties in the city and the Piraeus respectively; and above them thirty other officers with absolute powers. Some of these men happened to be relatives and acquaintances of mine, and they invited me to join them at once in what seemed to be a proper undertaking.

Xenophon (*Mem.* 9–16) focuses on what he implies are the expressed anti-democratic views of Socrates: 'he said that it was foolish for the archons of the state to be chosen by lot', as well as his responsibility for nurturing the ambitions of two associates, perhaps the greatest enemies of the democracy, Critias and Alcibiades: 'But, said the prosecutor, Critias and Alcibiades were associates of Socrates, and they wrought the greatest harm to the state. Critias was the most rapacious and violent of all in the oligarchy, while Alcibiades was the most intemperate and insolent man of all in the democracy' (12). In fact, Xenophon here is apparently quoting not from Meletus, but rather from a political pamphlet written by one Polycrates after the events in the courtroom (remember, the first books of his *Memorabilia* were written while in exile, long after the trial):[6] none of this could have come up at the actual trial; immunity applied to crimes committed before 402 BCE, the date of the amnesty, and political prosecutions were strictly out of order. Returning, then, to the likely strategy of Meletus and company, what better way to attack Socrates than through a charge of atheism?

'ATHEISM' AND 'IMPIETY' IN ATHENS: WAS SOCRATES AN 'ATHEIST'?

Perhaps the twenty-first century will serve to remind the reader of the extent to which issues of class, nationalism and religious fundamentalism can all become inextricably intertwined. Granted, fourth-century BCE Athens was very far from a theocracy and, for us, it may be difficult to imagine a state-sanctioned charge of atheism drawing the death penalty in a polytheistic society where there were no codified religious doctrines or canonical scriptures; where traditions about the gods were transmitted through what everyone agreed was the work of human poets, Homer and Hesiod; and where matters of *orthopraxis*, but not orthodoxy, would have determined one's conformity to the state-sponsored religion. What kind of evidence for Socrates' atheism would those acting on behalf of the state have been able to present at the trial? Meletus seems to turn Socrates into a reductive physicist: '[Meletus speaking] Gentlemen of the jury, he says that the sun is stone and the moon earth' (*Ap.* 26d33). Socrates says that here Meletus is confusing him with Anaxagoras, an Ionian philosopher whose books one could buy for a drachma at the local shop. More telling, perhaps, is the exclamation of Socrates himself; he exclaims to the jury: 'I believe in gods as do none of my accusers' (35d). What did Plato mean to signal by this avowed difference? Scholars have pointed to other dialogues such as the *Euthyphro*, whose theme is piety, and to *Republic* 377c–378d: both of these texts insist that traditions that represent the gods as harming each other or even disagreeing do not adequately convey what piety means or the nature of the gods in general. How can gods commit adultery, lie and do much pretty the kinds of things that the worst human beings do? Indeed, throughout Plato's dialogues, Socrates consistently maintains (as Xenophon's

Socrates does not) that the gods are only beneficial, that they are not responsible for any evil and that, if the gods love what is pious, then piety will have a single nature, not variable for different worshippers or different gods. As we saw above, however, although the language of the charge accuses Socrates of 'not believing in the gods the city believes in', it is hard to imagine a prosecution success of Socrates because he does not literally believe in the truth of every myth or, more generally, because he sees the gods as good and harmonious, as sources of all and only good things for human beings. The difficulty lies in determining to what extent mere matters of belief were liable to prosecution in the late fifth century BCE, as opposed to specific acts of sacrilege, such as profaning the mysteries.

To understand the role that religious conservatism played in the condemnation of Socrates, it will be necessary to address the larger question of intellectual persecution in the fifth and fourth centuries BCE. Evidence for this persecution is abundant, though much of it is later, as in this report from Plutarch:

> Men could not abide the natural philosophers (*physikoi*) and 'astronomaniacs' (*meteoroleschai*), as they were then called, because they reduced the divine agency down to irrational causes, blind forces, and necessary incidents. Even Protagoras had to go into exile, Anaxagoras was with difficulty rescued from imprisonment by Pericles, and Socrates, although he had nothing whatever to do with such matters, nevertheless lost his life because of philosophy. (*Life of Nicias* 23.2–3)

In fact, while some scholars have tried to develop the case that there was a steady rise not only in intellectual experimentation during the decades preceding Socrates' execution but also in Athenian juridical reaction to such innovation, recently there has been a tendency to downplay the historicity of the five or six cases of prosecution for impiety that allegedly took place and set the precedent for Socrates' trial and conviction. One bit of evidence concerns the 'decree of Diopeithes', perhaps passed in the 430s BCE, which outlawed those whom Plutarch (a first-century CE Roman writer) referred to as 'showing disrespect regarding the divine things' and as 'teaching about the celestial phenomena', that is atheists and astrologers (*Pericles* 32). Attestations to this decree are found only centuries after it was allegedly was passed, and, in particular, the legal language of the decree as reported by Plutarch has been doubted.

Other evidence for the phenomenon of religious persecution is also suspect: for example, Diogenes Laertius reports that the Sophist Protagoras, antihero of two Platonic dialogues, the *Protagoras* and the *Theaetetus*, arrived in Athens and promptly read a work titled *On Gods*; evidently the first sentence read, 'as to the gods, I have no means of knowing either that they exist or that they do not exist.' According to Plutarch's story, the Athenians were so incensed by this treatise that they immediately expelled Protagoras and burned copies of his books in the *agora*. However, Plato himself indicates no such outrage or outlawing; in fact, in the *Meno*, Plato says the opposite: '[Protagoras] was nearly seventy when he died and had practiced his craft for forty years. During all that time to this very day his reputation has stood high' (91e). Another alleged victim of religious persecution was the pre-Socratic philosopher Anaxagoras, to whom, as we saw, Socrates alludes in *Apology* 26d: 'Do you think you are accusing Anaxagoras?' Again, Socrates makes no mention of a trial for impiety in his defence speech, though it would perhaps have been odd for him to cite Anaxagoras if indeed the latter had provided the antecedent for his legal case. However, Diogenes Laertius, writing over six centuries later and relying on late authors (II.12), reports that Anaxagoras was 'prosecuted for impiety by Cleon and defended by his disciple, Pericles'.

Perhaps the only clear evidence we have of such a charge of impiety being successfully prosecuted is the case of Diagoras of Melos, who in 414 BCE was wanted by the Athenians, dead or alive, for the crime of defaming the Eleusinian mysteries. We learn of his escape from Athens from jokes in Aristophanes' *Birds*. At *Clouds* 828–30, after the initiation ceremonies that take place in the 'Think-o-mat', the naive Strepsiades learns that Zeus is out of fashion and accordingly instructs his son:

STREPSIADES: Dinos is king, now he's driven out Zeus . . .

PHIDIPPIDES: Who says so?

STREPSIADES: Socrates the Melian.

Aristophanes here is equating Socrates and Diagoras. According to one scholar, Diagoras must have enraged the Athenians on account of his writings. According to this same scholar we now possibly possess a treatise by Diagoras of Melos in the form of the Derveni Papyrus, discovered in 1962 in the remains of a funeral pyre in northern Greece. For Janko, this scroll 'is a copy of a treatise written within Socrates' lifetime, as its style proves beyond any doubt'.[7] Moreover, its likely author, Diagoras of Melos, would have been guilty of profaning the Orphic mysteries by subjecting the Orphic theogonical poem to allegorical interpretation. Janko summarizes the significance of the find for our subject as follows:

> By reinterpreting the Orphic cosmogony and mocking the Orphic initiates in column 20 of the text, Diagoras would have made his audiences question whether it was worth the trouble and expense of getting initiated. . . . The ultimate outrage would have been the allegory itself – the interpretation of the holy poem as a coded version of the latest physics, and the equation of God with a material element, Air.

The theology of Diagoras – and of others of this particular philosophical enclave, who included Diogenes of Apollonia and, some scholars believe, Socrates himself – is important for the story that is beginning to unfold. Let us review the relevant facts to see whether, somehow, we can make sense of the religious side of Socratic thought. In the first place, we saw that the *Clouds* assimilated Socrates' thought to a form of natural philosophy espoused by his contemporary Diagoras of Melos, who represents, in a sense, the last gap of truly pre-Socratic Ionian speculation. According to Diagoras, in agreement with another contemporary – Diogenes of Apollonia – Zeus can be equated with the element air. Both philosophers, like Anaxagoras, were material monists: air is the universal 'underlying stuff' (Sedley 2008, 76).

Let's compare fragment B5 of Diogenes, contemporary of Socrates and also of Aristophanes, with the *Clouds'* cosmology. First, Diogenes:

> It seems to me that the thing that possesses intelligence is what people call air, and that it is by this that everybody is governed, and that it controls everything. For this thing seems to me itself to be a god, to extend everywhere, to dispose everything, and to be present in everything.

Now, *Clouds*:

> Impossible! I'd never come up with a single thing about celestial
> phenomena, if I did not suspend my mind up high, to mix my
> subtle thoughts with what's like them (274–8)
>   O Sovereign Lord, O Boundless Air (318)
>   No – they're heavenly Clouds, great goddesses . . . from them we
> get our thoughts. (389–90)

The parallels are striking: we are dealing with a material element that
is also divine; what governs the world as a whole is also present in
human beings as mind.

Now, what Diogenes accomplishes is perhaps less than what some
have claimed for him, according to the most recent analysis of the
fragments, although it is still considerable: he shows that the underlying material principle of the universe is intelligent and that what
intelligence does is arrange things for the best (Sedley 2008, 78).

Before we close this chapter on the charges of atheism against
Socrates, one more piece of evidence must be considered, and this is
the so-called intellectual autobiography of Socrates which Plato
recounts at *Phaedo* 97c1: 'one day I heard someone reading, as he
said, from a book of Anaxagoras, and saying that it is Mind that
directs and is the cause of everything.' Later, however, Socrates
evinces his disappointment in the physics of Anaxagoras because the
latter evidently failed to assign Mind a teleological role in the ordering of the universe; instead, Anaxagoras 'gave [Mind] no responsibility
for the management of things, but mentioned as causes air and water'
(98c1).

The upshot is perhaps more astonishing than we might realize; in
fact, it seems that it is Socrates who is searching for a universal cause, a
god, if you will, who orders and arranges things for the best. Xenophon's
Memorabilia, a source that we shall consider in more detail below, has
Socrates explain just this conception of deity in two passages, in conversations that Xenophon swears he heard in person. In one passage,
Socrates appears to give the very first argument from intelligent design
to demonstrate the existence of an intelligent creator god:

> Compare things with regard to which there is no sign of what they
> are for, and things which evidently serve a beneficial purpose.

Which ones do you judge to be the products of change, and which of design? (I.4.2)

The irony here is that, far from embracing the materialist monism attributed to him by Aristophanes and associated with Diogenes and Diagoras, Socrates can be seen as the advocate of a distinctively unscientific theology – an innovation to be sure, but very far from atheism (Sedley 2008, 82).

In the Platonic dialogues, Socrates treads a dangerous line between association with the Sophists by frequenting their lectures, reading their books and appearing in public with them, and simultaneously distinguishing his own profession, philosophy, from theirs, Sophistry. Indeed, it could be said that one of Plato's projects in writing the dialogues that feature Socrates in conversation with a number of Sophists (*Protagoras, Hippias Major, Gorgias*) was to make the case that Socrates was the very antithesis of a Sophist and that philosophy differed in every respect from its counterpart, rhetoric. In the same way, Plato seems to make Socrates at the very least familiar with the Ionian physicists; from this, we should not make the same mistake as Aristophanes: Socrates was no scientist. Instead, what was controversial in Socrates' religious thinking was his belief in a deity that created, acted and governed for the best; this deity could never, therefore, be the cause of detriment or harm, even to one's enemies.

SOCRATES THE MARTYR: SOCRATES' DEATH AND ITS MEANING IN HISTORY

Out of the shadows of Socrates' death, Plato creates a silhouetted figure, the philosopher Socrates; his preoccupation with Socrates only grows in the dialogues, where this silhouette takes on life and develops an interior but, above all, takes on a voice. Socrates poses among Sophists but is not one: he studies the physicists and is even mistaken for one, more than once. He dies from an overdetermination of causes: atheism, mistaken identity, comic malice spilling out of control; bad company; a supercilious personality, a victim of blanket fundamentalism or a unique target, the first martyr to philosophy.

The legacy of Socrates, therefore, is as much in his death as in his life. Perhaps this is another way that Socrates is paradigmatic. As Mark Edwards writes:

Nothing, 'with one exception', said the Reverend Benjamin Jowett, resembles the death of Socrates in Plato [Jowett 1892, 194]. . . . George Steiner observe[d] that our 'moral and intellectual history' is characterized by two deaths, each of which is preceded by a famous supper. [Steiner 1996, 391–2; 399].[8]

Edwards' essay, 'Socrates and the early Church', demonstrates the 'neglect of the living Socrates' in favour of what arguably became an obsession in the centuries after he lived: his death. Early Christians compared the death of Socrates to the sacrifice of Jesus, as in this passage from Justin Martyr's (second-century CE) second *Apology*:

> And those who by human birth were more ancient than Christ, when they attempted to consider and prove things by reason, were brought before the tribunals as impious persons and busybodies. And Socrates, who was more zealous in this direction than all of them, was accused of the very same crimes as ourselves. For they said that he was introducing new divinities, and did not consider those to be gods whom the state recognized. But he cast out from the state both Homer and the rest of the poets, and taught men to reject the wicked demons and those who did the things which the poets related; and he exhorted them to become acquainted with the God who was to them unknown, by means of the investigation of reason . . .

Justin Martyr used the prestige of the Classical philosophical tradition and the martyrdom of Socrates on behalf of reason itself (*logos*, the Greek word for 'reason', is also obviously the Logos of Christ) in his *First Apology* and *Second Apology*, addressed respectively to Antoninus Pius and the Roman Senate. These are defence speeches that picked up accusations made against the Christians by recalling the charge of atheism made against Socrates, depicted here as a proto-Christian. The death of Socrates reverberated even in the Islamic world, as translations of Plato and possibly Xenophon as well as Diogenes Laertius made their way into the Arabic tradition.[9] Al-Kindi, usually thought of as the first Arab philosopher (d. 873 CE), wrote a number of treatises about Socrates, most of which are now lost (although Adamson 2007 has recently discussed a text from a gnomological collection titled 'What al-Kindi reported from the sayings of Socrates').

According to Alon, Socrates' death is related in two different summaries in Arabic of the *Phaedo* and *Crito*, while Socrates himself is celebrated as a 'prophet', 'as an ideal for Muslim holy men'; indeed, Islam has its own tradition of religious martyrs. One such, Suhrawardi al-Maqtul (the Slain), who was born in 1154 CE in Iran and executed in 1191 CE on the orders of Salah al-Din, on charges of corrupting the religion, was perhaps inevitably compared to Socrates (Alon 2006).

The death of Socrates inspired literary imitations and artistic representations especially in the French Enlightenment, as *littérateurs* belonging to the age of *philosophes* celebrated Socrates in the battle against censorship, even as the subject of Socrates' death became enormously popular in painting.[10] Diderot (d. 1784), the beleaguered encyclopedist, translated Plato's *Apology* into French while imprisoned for his atheistic pamphlet, *Lettre sur les aveugles*. Voltaire invoked the name of Socrates in a letter to Diderot concerning the case of a young 'blasphemer' (Jean-François de la Barre) who was mutilated and beheaded and then burned on a funeral pyre along with a copy of Voltaire's *Dictionnaire philosophique*. He wrote 'one simply has to write to Socrates [i.e. Diderot] when the Meletuses and Anytuses are soaked in blood and are lighting fires at the stake' (Goulbourne 2007, 229–30).[11]

If the name of Socrates in antiquity conjured up a picture of the snub-nosed, pot-bellied, balding Satyr-like being described in Plato's *Symposium* and *Theaetetus*, for the moderns the image that comes to mind is more likely to be that of David's *Socrate au moment de prendre la cigüe* ('Socrates at the moment of taking the hemlock'), painted in 1787, a work that joined a number of other renderings of Socrates' death in the second half of the eighteenth century.[12] The painting does not actually depict his death, but rather the moment before Socrates' death, as Socrates points upwards towards heaven, reflecting his discourse about the immortality of the soul in the *Phaedo*. It succeeds in conveying the theme of the *Phaedo*, the philosopher's fearless pursuit of death, while its deployment in print came to symbolize 'the more specifically political connotations of the persecuted victim of an unjust ruling faction'.[13]

We today count perhaps one fact among all of the fictions surrounding Socrates, his drinking of hemlock in an Athenian prison, just as the death of Jesus is another monumental cultural fact, whatever we make of it (we saw Jowett make this very point). However morbidly inspiring or possibly encouraging this story and image of the dying Socrates have become for us, it is now time to turn to the life of Socrates.

FURTHER READING

Alon, I. 1995. *Socrates Arabus*. Jerusalem: Hebrew University. A study of Socrates in Arabic literature.

Brickhouse, T. and Smith, N. 1994. *Plato's Socrates*. Oxford: Oxford University Press. A good resource for general issues surrounding the trial and execution of Socrates.

Kerferd, G. B. 1981. *The Sophistic Movement*. Cambridge: Cambridge University Press.

Nehamas, A. 1998. *The Art of Living*. Berkeley; Los Angeles, CA: University of California Press. Nehamas devotes a section of his book to the subject of Montaigne's relationship to Socrates.

Sedley, D. 2008. *Creationism and Its Critics in Antiquity*. Berkeley; Los Angeles, CA: University of California Press. Sedley examines the theology of the late fifth century BCE as it relates to the testimonies of Plato and Xenophon.

Stone, I. F. 1989. *The Trial of Socrates*. New York: Anchor Books. An overview of the politics behind the trial of Socrates.

Wilson, E. 2007. *The Death of Socrates*. Princeton, NJ: Princeton University Press. An extended meditation on the death of Socrates.

CHAPTER THREE

THE SOURCES FOR SOCRATES

OVERVIEW OF THE SOURCES

Now it is time to turn to a more detailed investigation of the relative merits of the competing portraits of Socrates, with the caveat that we may not succeed in distinguishing thereby the 'real' Socrates who lurks among a number of imposters, although we shall understand the enormous interest generated by the figure of Socrates in the fourth century BCE. In looking for traces of the historical Socrates, we turn, as noted in chapter one, to the writings of the Socratics that began to circulate in the 390s BCE and continued to be published into the mid-part of the fourth century BCE; thus, we can imagine Plato writing the *Apology* some time after the events of 399 BCE, while, at the other extreme, Xenophon is thought to have finished his *Memorabilia,* or *Recollections,* of Socrates as late as 355 BCE, after returning from a 30-year absence from Athens.[1] In addition to the more complete sets of Socratic writings (Plato's Socratic dialogues and Xenophon's *Memorabilia* in four books, as well as his *Symposium*) we possess very incomplete remains of Socratic dialogues written by other members of the Socratic circle, including Antisthenes, Aeschines and Phaedo. These three Socratics, at any rate, will be the subject of a survey later in this chapter. With the exception of the *Clouds*, the only other source of information we have about Socrates comes from the testimonial of Aristotle, but, as we shall see below, it is doubtful that much in these remarks is independent of what Aristotle found in the Socratic works of Plato.

SOCRATES IN ARISTOPHANES' *CLOUDS*

Already we have spent some time with the *Clouds* of 424 BCE and have seen the difficulties it presents for the current enterprise. If we regard this play as too unreliable to tell us anything about Socrates both because, as a caricature, this Aristophanic portrait is painted with too broad a stroke and because the picture of Socrates painted seems, on first glance, so unfamiliar, then we must sacrifice this source, the only such text actually published during the lifetime of Socrates.[2] It is up to the reader to decide, on the basis of the available evidence, how credible the play may be. Anyone reading the play for the first time will be delighted with the figure of Socrates: pale, in rags, flea-bitten, starving and circling about in grand style above the 'Think-o-mat', presiding over the mysteries taught therein and piously, if inconsistently, worshipping the majestic Clouds, the goddesses of the *phrontisterion*:

STREPSIADES: That is the Think-shop of sage souls. There dwell men

Who maintain the heaven's a snuffer and we men coals. They teach (if you pay them) how to win any case, Right or Wrong.

PHEIDIPPIDES: Who are they?

STREPSIADES: I don't rightly know the name, but they are deep thinkers and fine gentlemen.

PHEIDIPPIDES: They're scoundrels. I know them. You mean those impostors, pale and barefoot. That miserable Socrates is one. Chaerephon another (*Clouds* 94–104 Hadas trans.).

Later in the play, when Socrates is made to introduce his 'theology', he says that the goddesses he worships are the sources of 'acumen, and casuistry, verbal sleights, circumlocutions, quick repartee and knockout arguments (*Clouds* 315 Hadas trans.).

The Socrates depicted in this play engages in two very different kinds of activities; he seems to be a devotee of cosmological speculation of the kind normally associated with Ionian physicists, explaining natural phenomena in terms of their material components and simultaneously rejecting the traditional gods: 'What Zeus? Don't be silly; there is no Zeus' (*Clouds* 366 Hadas trans.).

However, the deities he worships are in effect patrons of the Sophists, the group, who, as we saw in the previous chapter, wandered to Athens from abroad in search of wealthy pupils who would enlist in enrol expensive courses, hoping to learn persuasive techniques in order to advance in political careers.[3] The play ends on this topic, with the debate between right and wrong, as they are translated sometimes, or, more literally, between just and unjust discourse, to whose tutelage Socrates abandons Strepsiades (the hero of the play, who enrols in the 'Think-o-mat' to evade his creditors), because he has proved so intractable a student. The unjust discourse borrows from the 'maxims' of the Sophists, while advancing typically comic motivations combined with bawdy humour, as in the following exchange:

UNJUST DISCOURSE: I am logic.

JUST DISCOURSE: But the worse.

UNJUST DISCOURSE: Still I'll beat you, who claim to be my better.

JUST DISCOURSE: What device will you use?

UNJUST DISCOURSE: New notions I invent.

JUST DISCOURSE: Such stuff succeeds with the fools out there.

(He points to the audience.)

UNJUST DISCOURSE: No, the wise.

JUST DISCOURSE: I'll lay you out.

UNJUST DISCOURSE: Tell me, doing what?

JUST DISCOURSE: Speaking what's just.

UNJUST DISCOURSE: And I'll smother it by speaking the contrary. There's no such thing as justice, say I.

JUST DISCOURSE: You say there's not?

UNJUST DISCOURSE: Where is it, tell me.

JUST DISCOURSE: With the gods.

UNJUST DISCOURSE: Then why, if there's justice, was Zeus not ruined for tying his father up?

JUST DISCOURSE: Faugh! I'm getting nauseous: give me a basin.

UNJUST DISCOURSE: You're a broken down spastic driveler.
(*Clouds* 892–906 Hadas trans.)

What we can say about the Sophists – a group of people who popu- late the Socratic dialogues and with whom Socrates most often clashes – is that they tended to share certain characteristics, including teaching for pay, being itinerant, being involved with politics, writing treatises and publishing them, and giving formal instruction in forensic and epideictic rhetoric. One feature of Sophistic teaching is the subject of opposition everywhere in the Socratic dialogues, in which we meet Socrates interrogating the views of characters such as Protagoras (*Theaetetus*), Hippias (*Hippias Major*), Thrasymachus (*Republic* I) and Gorgias (*Gorgias*), and this is what one scholar has called, 'Sophistic ethics' (Bett 2002). Sophistic ethics tends to employ two fundamental strategies: the first is to suggest that moral values vary across cultures, over time, and among individuals and groups, so that there are no moral absolutes; the second exploits the implicit contrast between conventions, or *nomos* (not universal), and nature, or *phusis* (universal), to suggest that by nature individuals seek their own advantage, whereas law or convention inhibits this capacity. Both of these strategies were deployed in contexts that appeared highly subversive of traditional values.

Evidence of this rough configuration that we are calling Sophistic ethics exists in independently surviving treatises, including a treatise titled *Dissoi Logoi*, evidently an instruction manual for arguing on both sides of a position. Statements such as the following are alarming, but, in fact, Socrates himself argues (*Mem.* IV.3; *R* I) that sometimes 'it is just to deceive'.

1. Twofold arguments are also put forward concerning the just and the unjust. And some say that the just is one thing and the unjust another, and others that the just and the unjust are the same. And I shall try to support this latter view.
2. And in the first place I shall argue that it is just to tell lies and to deceive. (III I, 1–2: Sprague trans. *Mind* 306, 155–67)

Another example of what is apparently a denial of the stable identity of justice, or even its reality, consistent with what we saw uttered by the Unjust Discourse, may be found in the fragments of work by Antiphon the Sophist:

Bearing true witness for one another is regarded as just and no less as useful for human pursuits. Now, whoever does this will not be just, if it is just to wrong no one and not be wronged oneself. For one who bears witness, even if his testimony is true, must nevertheless somehow wrong another . . . and be wronged himself inasmuch as the one testified against is convicted because of the testimony given by him, and loses either his money or his life because of this man to whom he does no wrong. Now in this he wrongs the one testified against, in that he harms one who is not wronging him; and he is himself wronged by the one testified against, in that he is hated by him for bearing true witness.[4]

Now, we saw that Socrates emphatically denies sharing any of the more external traits of the Sophists: he is a native Athenian; he does not teach for a fee. But more importantly, Socrates goes out of his way to combat precisely these Sophistic strategies and pointedly argues against them on many occasions: that virtue is the same for all, for men, women, citizens and slaves; that doing injustice is something that the doer thereof would find intrinsically undesirable. Nevertheless, some of the paradoxes, the sayings famously associated with Socrates, have an air of Sophisms about them. In chapter six, we shall have the opportunity to explore the Socratic paradoxes. For now, we can note that, for example, the doctrine associated with Socrates, that no one errs willingly appears, on the surface, to deny moral culpability. The Sophist Gorgias suggests in a surviving treatise, the *Encomium of Helen*, that wrongdoing in general, and Helen's wrongdoing in particular (a brief reminder to the reader: she commits adultery with Paris), is involuntary:

> For it was logos that persuaded her soul, and she who was persuaded was compelled both to obey what was suggested and to approve of the deeds (proposed) whereas the argument that persuaded her does commit injustice, on the grounds that it compels her.[5]

In chapter six, again, we shall look at some of the Socratic paradoxes, in the light of Sophistic theses, to see how Socrates often uses Sophistic arguments in order to defeat the theses. For now, we note the strong associations between Socrates and the Sophists revealed in the second half of the *Clouds*.

THE SOCRATIC CIRCLE AND THE SOCRATIC LITERATURE

Turning now from what has too long engaged us, the value of Aristophanes as a character witness to Socrates, we consider the evidence offered by surviving fragments from the genre known as 'Socratic literature'. Book two of Diogenes Laertius' *Lives of the Eminent Philosophers* suggests that fully 12 members of the Socratic circle wrote dialogues: Xenophon, Aeschines, Aristippus, Theodorus, Phaedo, Eucleides, Stilpo, Crito, Simon, Glaucon, Simmias and Cebes. The majority of fragments from these Socratics have been collected in a four-volume work, *Socratis et Socraticorum Reliquiae* (*SSR*); other fragments are available elsewhere.[6] Only a brief survey of some of these writers is possible in this space.

ANTISTHENES AND THE CYNICS

Antisthenes[7] (445–365 BCE; compare with Plato, 428–347 BCE) is considered the oldest of the Socratics.[8] Just as important, though, is Xenophon's depiction of him in the *Symposium* (4.57–64; 8.4–6), where Antisthenes appears as a close associate, even a fanatical devotee, of Socrates. As we'll see in chapter seven, when we discuss the Socratic schools in more detail. Antisthenes resembles several other followers of Socrates insofar as he is traditionally made out to be the founder of another branch of philosophy,[9] in his case the Dogs, or Cynic philosophers. Diogenes Laertius records the now almost universally rejected scholastic succession of the Cynic-Stoic branch of the Socratic family: Socrates, Antisthenes, Diogenes, Crates, Zeno:

> He used to hold discussions in the gymnasium at Cynosarges not far from the gates, whence some [conclude] that the Cynic school derived its name from that district. . . . And he was the first . . . to double his cloak and be content with that one garment and to take up a staff and a wallet. (DL)

Here the Socratic Antisthenes is said to inaugurate a particular lifestyle associated with Cynic philosophy, their practice of what may be called secular mendicancy. For this purpose, they assumed a trademark appearance. We have already seen that this device of wearing suitable philosophical attire is not unique to the Cynics, if we are to believe both Plato and Aristophanes. For evidently those who styled themselves Socratics also affected a certain look – pale and thin, according to Aristophanes, or barefoot, according to Plato (*Clouds* 1017; *Symp.* 173b2).

Our interest is particularly in Antisthenes' ethics, for the reason that, as discussed above, part of what it meant to be a Socratic was to be a follower of Socrates, to imitate his life. Antisthenes is said to have taught that 'evil is constituted by everything that is foreign' (DL vi.12), a doctrine we find elaborated in Epictetus' *Dissertationes* 3.24.67 (*SSR* VB 22):

> Since the time Antisthenes set me free I have no longer been a slave . . . he taught me [the distinction between] what is mine and what is not mine. Property is 'not mine'. Relatives, servants, friends, reputation, accustomed haunts, pastimes, [he taught] are foreign.

Xenophon represents a conversation between Antisthenes and Socrates on the subject of inner wealth: 'it is not in their houses that human beings keep their wealth or their poverty, but in their souls' (Symposium 4.36; *SSR* VA 82). Socrates famously offers his own poverty (*Ap.* 23c1; 31c3)[10] as evidence that he does not take pay for teaching, that he is not a Sophist. Surely Socrates' example of neglecting matters of business, his refusal to see his good in creating external wealth, is a part of his ethical teaching that extended into the Cynics' well-known homelessness and practice of self-reliance. What this link suggests, then, is that Socrates' life itself gave rise to philosophical reflection on the meaning of that life. In the *Memorabilia*, Xenophon portrays Socrates and Antisthenes as practitioners of self-reliance, exhibiting the tough, pragmatic, anti-hedonistic bent of Socrates' own life. As is true of Socrates, part of Antisthenes' teaching style consisted in the utterance of apothegms – cryptic barbs that packed a punch, going right to the heart of the matter. One such saying attributed to Antisthenes is 'I would rather go mad than feel pleasure'. We will have much more to say about the topic of pleasure and how it figures into Socratic ethics, as reported by both Plato and Xenophon. For now, we can advance the testimony concerning Antisthenes, together with several of his reported sayings, to suggest that for the Socratic circle, the life of Socrates was an object of imitation; Socratic philosophy, in addition to its theoretical elements, if such there were, was at least a way of life.[11]

AESCHINES

Insofar as we have access to stories and anecdotes depicting the Socratic way of life from other members of the circle, we begin to develop a kind of composite portrait – similar to the way a police artist works to render a face from the accounts of several eyewitnesses. Another useful writer to read for clues about Socrates' philosophy is Aeschines. We are fortunate to possess several of his dialogues, including his version of an Alcibiades (Plato wrote the *Symposium*, which contains the story of Socrates and Alcibiades, and the *First Alcibiades*: a record of their first encounter). 'The only thing I say I know', Socrates tells us in the *Symposium*, 'is the art of love' (177d8–9). Socrates was notorious for his friendships with beautiful young men; indeed, Alcibiades was reportedly linked erotically to Socrates, at least in some way, and, as it happens, was a famous beauty in the days of his friendship with Socrates. That this emblematic romance might not even be original with Plato, and that Plato might have been elaborating on an Aeschinean version already circulating, makes the story, with its multiple retellings in Plato (the *Symposium* and the *Alcibiades* dialogues), all the more compelling as evidence for the meaning of Socratic eros.[12] In Aeschines' *Alcibiades*, Socrates is made to confess his love for Alcibiades and offers to explain his motives for associating with him.

> Because of the love that I truly felt for Alcibiades, I suffered an experience no different from that of the Maenads. Indeed, when the Maenads become full of the god, they are able to draw milk and honey from wells from which others cannot even draw water. So it is with me, although I have no wisdom that I can teach and so benefit the man, nevertheless I imagined that I could make him better through associating with him, on account of my love. [13]

The Socratic life involved not only the philosopher–disciple relationship, which seems rather conventional, but a charismatic attraction that Socrates had for his young followers and the acknowledgement that, at least in some way, Socrates reciprocated this attraction. It is the unique accomplishment of the Socratic literature to feature this dimension of Socratic teaching while showing that friendship and love are in themselves made topics for philosophical discussion. Socrates was not just a friend, although he was certainly that; he was also a philosopher of friendship. On this, virtually all of our witnesses agree. The Aeschines fragment agrees with Plato and Xenophon not only in portraying Socrates as investigating the philosophical grounds of friendship, but also in revealing the powerful effects of the Socratic encounter. Socrates approaches Alcibiades with the intention of removing his arrogance. Socrates reveals his broader technique at *Lysis* 210e2, when he instructs Hippothales on the way to capture Lysis, a youth with whom Hippothales has fallen in love: 'this is how you should talk to your boyfriends, Hippothales, making them humble and drawing in their sails, instead of swelling them up and spoiling them, as you do' (210e2–5). Socrates' aim in Aeschines' *Alcibiades* is precisely to allow Alcibiades a share of Socrates' own awareness of his fundamental ignorance about virtue. Socrates compels 'Alcibiades to weep, laying his head on his lap, thinking that he was not even close to Themistocles in his preparation [to rule the city]'. (Aeschines fr. 53)

PHAEDO OF ELIS AND THE *ZOPYRUS*

In chapter ten of Cicero's *De fato*, we read of an encounter between Socrates and Zopyrus, a Persian physiognomer who visits Athens and claims that he is able to read the character of a person from his countenance.[14] When Zopyrus meets Socrates, he pronounces the latter 'stupid, dull and . . . also a womanizer'. In his reply, Socrates admits that although these are quite possibly his native vices, he has been able to uproot them. This tale is related in one of two dialogues attributed to Phaedo of Elis, a member of the Socratic circle and most famously the companion portrayed in Plato's eponymous dialogue. Socrates here is made to recognize a colleague, a professional who studies human nature. But it is only owing to his self-knowledge that Socrates can admit, before an audience of his admirers, that Zopyrus is an adept. One of the themes treated in this tantalizingly brief quotation from the *Zopyrus*, a dialogue that was read well into late antiquity, is the extent to which both Socrates and Zopyrus, who are engaged in the same profession, diagnosing the condition of the human soul, rely on their clients' self-knowledge for confirmation of their skills. Again, there is a kind of universal agreement among the Socratic authors that self-knowledge, rather than knowledge of states of affairs in the world, whether politics, scientific facts or matters of artistic expertise, was the particular focus of Socratic philosophy.

THE SOURCES FOR SOCRATES

For example, in the *Phaedrus*, Socrates says that he has no time for investigating myths, since he does not as yet 'Know himself' (230).

Thus far we have been tracing thematic elements in the Socratic literature, including erotically charged philosophical friendship, the cultivation of virtue through self-knowledge, and Socrates' practice of external and internal poverty. Perhaps more than any systematic ethics, we have seen that all of this literature focuses on the Socratic life, sometimes even self-consciously, as in the example of the *Zopyrus*, where we have a physiognomer literally reading the face of Socrates to us, the intended audience, to give us a picture of the inner man. In the previous chapter, we studied the importance of Socrates' death; what we see in this chapter is something more important, the living example of Socrates. Having begun this survey with the oldest portrait of Socrates, we turn finally to the youngest Socratic, Xenophon (431–355 BCE), author of four works that are explicitly Socratic, the *Memorabilia, Symposium, Apology of Socrates* and *Estate Manager*. We have had occasion to mention some of these works already.

XENOPHON

The subject of Xenophon's Socratic credentials has been a point of contention among scholars engaged, as we are here, in tracing Socratic literature to its original source, Socrates. Now is not the time to canvass all or even many of the opinions that, over the centuries, readers of Xenophon's Socratic works have formed of the man and his writings. But it is hard to resist giving some indication of how Xenophon fits into the history, not so much of philosophy, as of philosophical taste. Bertrand Russell said of Xenophon, in remarks of which not a few of his readers slyly approve:

> Let us begin with Xenophon, a military man, not very liberally endowed with brains, and on the whole conventional in his outlook. . . . There has been a tendency to think that everything Xenophon says must be true, because he had not the wits to think of anything untrue. This is a very invalid line of argument. A stupid man's report of what a clever man says is never accurate, because he unconsciously translates what he hears into something that he can understand. (Waterfield 1999, 80, quoting Russell)

Of course, it is unfair to study Xenophon via this insidious quote, yet it alerts us to the difficulties we face in evaluating the portrait of Socrates that Xenophon gives us. We must look at who the competition is: Plato. It is doubtful that any human being could stand up to such a comparison. This negative assessment of Xenophon's worth was not always the norm. Indeed, we saw that Schleiermacher assumed that Xenophon's Socrates was a good representation of the historical Socrates, so much so that he doubted the philosophical contribution of the man who has been called the founder of Western philosophy. In recent years, one prominent scholar has shown how important Xenophon's portrayal of Socrates was as a paradigm of ethics for what later became the Socratic schools, the Cynics and the Stoics.[15]

Of Xenophon himself, we know enough to frame his acquaintance with Socrates. He left Athens two years before Socrates' trial and execution to embark upon military service, along with ten thousand Greeks, to restore Cyrus the Younger to the throne of the Median Empire. Cyrus died in battle, and Xenophon, with the generals captured and slain, led these forces to safety through hostile Persian territory (hence, the *Anabasis*, or march upcountry). Xenophon reports that Socrates suggested he consult the Delphic Oracle about the advisability of this undertaking; later Socrates expresses his disapproval when Xenophon reports that he did not ask whether to join the expedition, but only which gods to supplicate for his success. He returned three years after the trial, but was then exiled for 30 years, perhaps for fighting under the command of the Spartans.

To what extent is this aristocrat, demonstrably obsessed with the values and station of an Athenian gentleman (in Greek, *kaloka-gathia*, a compound noun consisting of 'nobility' and 'moral worth'), an expatriate restored to Athens only late in life, in any way a Socratic, let alone a reliable informant about issues such as Socratic politics (if such there were), method or even ethics? Our approach will be to suspend judgement based on Xenophon's own life and, instead, to capture what for Xenophon is distinctive about the Socratic persona.

In his *Apology*, Xenophon makes Socrates a positive do-gooder, someone who strives to benefit his acquaintances by actively teaching them virtue, rather than, as in the Socratic dialogues, evidently withholding knowledge out of a profession to ignorance. Dorion (2006) summarizes this difference as follows:

1) Socrates X [X for Xenophon], who never avows ignorance of any moral subject, is capable of defining the virtues, while Socrates P [P for Plato], who claims to be ignorant of the most important subjects, tries in vain to define the virtues. Thus Socrates P must always begin his quest anew, while Socrates X never gives the impression of being at a loss for an answer to any question he asks.
2) Socrates X openly acknowledges that he is a teacher and an educational expert, while Socrates P, who denies being anyone's teacher,[16] often represents himself as his interlocutor's student.

It is this preceptor image that readers tend to find so tedious: Socrates tells his charges to avoid gluttony and can even get very specific about table manners (*Mem.* 3.14.1), to keep their hands off beautiful young men, and to be industrious and frugal. When reading the *Memorabilia*, we might appreciate the practical advice and agree with Xenophon that Socrates was 'very useful', but wonder, after all, whether this is a philosophy worth dying for. The effect of intellectual ennui is only the more exacerbated on reading the *Estate Manager*: Socrates' dialogue with a wealthy landowner concerning the virtues necessary to generate material wealth. How far, indeed, we seem to have travelled from the celestial Socrates, pale and poverty stricken, whirling about the heavens. Xenophon's is a Socrates deliberately tamed and brought down to earth. In fact, Xenophon goes out of his way to apologize for any suspicion that Socrates might have drawn; concerning his scientific curiosity – what good is such 'information' that has no practical use? – he is made to say: 'such studies are capable of using up an entire human life and preventing many other useful kinds of learning' (*Mem.* 4.7.3 and 5). Even if there is room in one's life for science, there is the danger that such knowledge may lead to hubris and carelessness: people like Anaxagoras apparently think they are already masters of human affairs (*Mem.* 1.1.12).[17]

No doubt behind the more conventional veneer of a Socrates who does not threaten overmuch, and who is perhaps a tad too respectable, there is a thread of, if not philosophy, then certainly virtue ethics not just woven throughout Xenophon's explicitly Socratic works, but, in a broader way, exemplified by all of the heroes portrayed in Xenophon's entire corpus. We can summarize the virtues that Xenophon identifies as Socratic if we glance once more at his *Apology*, where Xenophon writes that 'Socrates was the freest man to live'. Freedom, that is self-reliance, and hence a complex of other traits – self-control, endurance and self-sufficiency – is the singular achievement of, as well as recommendation for, the Socratic way of life. Xenophon writes at the beginning of the *Memorabilia*:

> It also seems extraordinary to me that any people should have been persuaded that Socrates had a bad influence upon young men. Besides what I have said already, he was in the first place the most self-disciplined of men in respect of his sexual and other appetites; then he was most tolerant of cold and heat and hardships of all kinds; and finally he had so trained himself to be moderate in his requirements that he was very easily satisfied with very few possessions. (I. 2.2–3)

However, it would be remiss to leave the discussion of Xenophon's Socrates so imbalanced, as if the hero of the dialogues was merely an abstemious fellow (this he certainly was) who had no interest in others. On the contrary, Xenophon writes his *Memorabilia* and *Symposium* in sympathy with other representations of the erotic Socrates: 'he made [his associates] desire virtue and gave them hope that if they took care for themselves they would become gentlemen. And though he never professed to be a teacher he made his associates hope by imitating him to become so, since he was himself manifestly of this sort' (1.2.2–3).

Socrates' erotic repertoire is vast and, like the membership of his circle, includes all social gradations: matchmaking, courtship, procuring and even matrimony.

One compelling illustration of the Socratic method of seduction is to be found in Socrates' interview with Theodote, in which Socrates instructs a courtesan on the art of ensnaring devoted lovers, part of which depends on a tried and true, but secret, method of arousing men's desires, a method that he calls 'implanting hunger'.

> SOCRATES: And for your favours you will best win your friends if you suit your largess to their penury; for, mark you, the sweetest viands presented to a man before he wants them are apt to prove insipid, or, to one already sated, even nauseous; but create hunger, and even coarser stuff seems honey – sweet.

> THEODOTE: How then shall I create this hunger in the heart of my friends?

SOCRATES: In the first place you must not offer or make suggestion of your dainties to jaded appetites until satiety has ceased
and starvation cries for alms. Even then shall you make but a faint
suggestion to their want, with modest converse – like one who
would fain bestow a kindness . . . and lo! the vision fades and she
is gone – until the very pinch of hunger; for the same gifts have
then a value unknown before the moment of supreme desire.
(*Mem.* III.11.7–15)

Theodote's telling phrase, this 'crea[ting] hunger,' involves the arousal
of a supreme desire, in this case, for virtue and wisdom. The *Memora-*
bilia ends with a reprise of the Socratic method of recruitment,
seduction or even conversion, following closely the story of Euthydemus – a handsome and ambitious young man whom Socrates
apparently takes special pains to win over.[18] The stages of this courtship are familiar from virtually all of the Socratic literature: Socrates
first establishes a kind of rapport with the target – here Euthydemus,
but one can compare Lysis or Theaetetus in the Platonic dialogues of
the same names. The next stage involves, as we saw in the advice Socrates gives to Theodote, implanting a desire for wisdom in the youth,
and this depends on showing him his deficiencies.

We saw that Aeschines' dialogue *Alcibiades* ends as Socrates compels
'Alcibiades to weep, laying his head on [Socrates'] lap', lamenting his
woeful lack of competence. After showing how Socrates successfully
captures Euthydemus, Xenophon gives us a primer on Socratic education, revealing its methods, its theory and its contents. For readers of
Plato, it is precisely here that Xenophon's charms begin to fade: we are
told that Socrates 'avoided disturbing or confusing [Euthydemus] but
rather explained most simply and clearly the things he thought it most
necessary to know and best to practice' (*Mem.* IV.2.40).

Socrates instructs Euthydemus in the topics of divine providence
(IV.3), justice (IV.4), self-mastery (IV.5), and dialectic and the art of
definition (IV.6). Now, the very manner that Xenophon adopts in
introducing this account of Socratic teaching, promising simplicity
and clarity, sets the reader up for reading the material in these sections
in a straightforward way; we are least prepared here for the proverbial
Socratic irony. Certainly, in the story that Xenophon tells of Socrates'
conversation with the Sophist Hippias, the anecdote ends with the
rather insipid remark that 'the gods are satisfied that "right" and
"lawful" mean the same.' Xenophon approvingly says at this point:

'by this sort of conversation and conduct, he made those who came into contact with him better men.' At this point the reader can only reject the conclusion: surely the example of Socrates himself, lawfully and yet, unjustly and wrongfully executed, would be foremost in the minds of Xenophon's readers, as the entire *Memorabilia* is, as we saw, written for the purpose of vindicating Socrates. If there is no recourse to irony, then we are left with a whitewashing of Socrates such as defies credibility.

The suggestion that, beneath the 'McBlimp' mask of Xenophon's Socrates, with his programmatic instruction manual for disciples whose self-confidence has been sufficiently undermined and his stolidly pragmatic values, there may lurk a critique of business as usual has been made.[19] For example, one scholar notes that the tract *The Household Manager*, written ostensibly as a manual on farming, is actually a Socratic dialogue whose purpose is to interrogate the artificial values of *kalokagathia* and their materialist underpinnings. There are three allusions in the *Estate Manager* to Aristophanes' *Clouds*; one such reference has the unmistakable signature of Socratic irony. In the treatise, Socrates recounts to a young disciple, Critoboulos, a conversation he had with the exceedingly wealthy Isomachus, a man with a reputation for being 'truly good'. Socrates says: 'I don't see how it could be right for me to correct a man who is perfectly and truly good, when my reputation is of being a windbag with his head in the clouds' (11.3). Socrates plays the buffoon against Isomachus the businessman, who is earnest about money making; Xenophon makes much of a play on words that can mean either 'benefit' or 'profit'.

To return to the primer of Socratic teaching that we find at the end of the *Memorabilia*, the Socrates of the *Clouds* worshipped Vortex, a material element that is the cause of everything and endowed with intelligence. Again, Socrates in the *Memorabilia* avoids physics because of the arrogance implied in this discipline, which causes us to turn too readily from matters of real concern.

On the one hand, reading this material, we have the feeling that Xenophon is crimping Plato's Socrates turning his dialectical technique and search for definition, his elenctic examination of the interlocutor, and the hints of ethical or political theories into a kind of Cliff's Notes on Socrates. Yet, for all of his borrowing, in fact, the contrast with Plato's Socrates could not be more profound; even in the *Apology*, the work in which Plato goes out of his way to defend the honour and innocence of Socrates, Socrates is made to say:

'If any of [my interlocutors] turns out to be good or not, I cannot justly bear responsibility' (33b3).

FURTHER READING

Dorion, L.-A. 2003. *Mémorables/Xénophon*; texte établi par Michele Bandini; traduit par Louis-André Dorion. Paris: Les Belles Lettres. The extensive introductory chapter is a good resource on Xenophon's Socrates.

Kahn, C. H. 1996. *Plato and the Socratic Dialogue*. Cambridge: Cambridge University Press.

Nussbaum, M. 1980. 'Aristophanes and Socrates on learning practical wisdom'. *Yale Classical Studies* 26: 43–97. This is a well-known discussion of Aristophanes' *Clouds* and Socrates.

Vander Waerdt, P. (ed.) 1994. *The Socratic Movement*. Berkeley; Los Angeles, CA: University of California Press. Contains numerous articles on Xenophon.

CHAPTER FOUR

PLATO'S SOCRATES

THE DEVELOPMENTALIST, UNITARIAN AND PROLEPTIC APPROACHES

The greatest of the Socratic writers is Plato. Plato's literary portraits of Socrates are astonishingly convincing works of art that purport to let us overhear the very conversations that Socrates had in his most private moments – minutes before his death with his wife and infant son (*Phaedo*), alone in bed with a worldly youth (*Symposium*) – as well as more public moments – for example, his trial before a jury of 500 Athenian citizens (*Apology*). The sheer brilliance of Plato's dramatic success in portraying Socrates makes us wonder, is there anything genuinely Socratic in Plato's dialogues, either a character who resembles the historical Socrates or doctrines and methods with which the historical Socrates operated? This question has no definitive answer, but there are a number of responses that one can canvass in order to see more clearly the relationship between Plato's Socrates and someone whom we'll just call 'Socrates', that is the older associate of Plato who was executed in 399 BCE.

Generally, we can distinguish three approaches to this relationship, although many more nuanced positions exist within the interstices of what we shall call the developmentalist, Unitarian and proleptic ways of reading the dialogues.[1] For developmentalists, the Socrates of Plato's early dialogues at least, represents, the philosophical interests and methods of the historical Socrates. For Unitarians, all that we find in Plato's dialogues is Plato; Socrates is an important influence, so much so that he might be seen as a mouthpiece for Plato's philosophy. For proleptic readers, the differences between the philosophical scope of the elenctic dialogues and the longer, more expository dialogues can be explained as a publication strategy. Thus a proleptic reading of Plato can be a Unitarian reading: we can think that everything we read in the dialogues is a reflection of Plato, who devised, for example, different works for different audiences, published certain works as a reflection of concerns within his Academy, and so forth. A necessary entry point for this discussion is the matter of the dialogues' chronology, for considerations of when or in what order Plato wrote the dialogues are sometimes used to make the case for developmentalism, that is the hypothesis that Plato began to write very much under the influence of Socrates but with time gradually expressed criticisms of Socratic philosophy and then freely experimented with his own philosophical agenda, even venturing into philosophical territory that was largely unexplored by Socrates.

VLASTOS' 'DEVELOPMENTAL' INTERPRETATION OF PLATO'S SOCRATES

As we saw, the person who most powerfully formulated developmentalism and its primary claim, namely that the Socrates of Plato's early dialogues represents the historical Socrates at least in large measure, was Gregory Vlastos.[2] In his summary article 'Socrates contra Socrates in Plato', Vlastos set out the ten criteria that distinguish the Socrates represented in a group of dialogues that he identified as constituting the early works of Plato. First, let's list these criteria (using abbreviations different from those that Vlastos employed) for the $Socrates_h$ of these Socratic dialogues versus the $Socrates_p$ who shows up in what Vlastos thinks of as 'Platonic' writings.[3]

1. $Socrates_h$ is a moral philosopher; $Socrates_p$ is an epistemologist, a metaphysician, a cosmologist.
2. $Socrates_p$ has a 'grand theory', namely the theory of forms; $Socrates_h$ does not allude to this theory.
3. $Socrates_h$ pursues knowledge via the elenchus, his question-and-answer method, and his results are inevitably aporetic; $Socrates_p$ seeks 'demonstrative' knowledge, and his results are positive.
4. $Socrates_p$ has a tripartite psychology; $Socrates_h$ thinks that there is no such thing as motivational conflict within a person.
5. $Socrates_h$ is not interested in mathematics; $Socrates_p$ is a master of mathematics.

6. Socrates$_h$ is a populist; Socrates$_p$ is an elitist.
7. Socrates$_p$ has an elaborate statecraft; Socrates$_h$ is critical of the democracy, but does not propose any alternative form of governance.
8. Socrates$_h$ is seen most often in company with a group of attractive youths; Socrates$_p$ explains erotic relationships in terms of a metaphysical and psychological theory.
9. Socrates$_h$ is pious and understands deity as 'rigorously ethical', as incapable of harm; Socrates$_p$ is a contemplative mystic.
10. Socrates$_h$ pursues philosophical question through adversarial conversation with interlocutors who disagree with him, sometimes most vehemently, the elenchus; Socrates$_p$ is didactic, expounding complex truths to interlocutors who serve as his 'yes' men.

What typifies the Socrates of the so-called Socratic dialogues, then, is a search for definitions of moral terms, the cardinal virtues recognized in traditional Greek culture. In the *Charmides*, Socrates asks a promising and physically stunning youth (who later turns out to be a member of the Thirty), 'what is modesty?' In the *Laches*, Socrates asks a pair of generals, Laches and Nicias, of whom the latter is, in terms of the dramatic date of the dialogue, about to lead a doomed and disastrous military campaign against Sicily, 'what is courage?' And in the *Euthyphro*, a dialogue that opens with Socrates standing before the king-archon's office to receive his official indictment on charges of impiety, Socrates asks a soothsayer, 'what is piety?' Sometimes the adversaries in these dialogues are a little more fierce, as in the *Gorgias*, where Socrates confronts a series of ever tougher opponents, each one more savagely defending the life of *pleonexia*, of rapaciousness, than the next. But in all of these dialogues, Socrates is relegated to the status of one who merely questions others' views; he offers no substantive philosophical views of his own and even disavows having any ethical knowledge.

Vlastos' identification of the Socratic persona in the aporetic dialogues[4] with the historical Socrates rests on the developmental hypothesis, according to which these dialogues are all early. Plato wrote them while still under the spell, as it were, of the master. The next group of dialogues, again for Vlastos, are transitional: here we see the same format, but there are hints of doctrines and philosophical interests that go beyond the almost purely destructive work of the dialogues of definition in which Socrates elicits a definition from mostly unwitting interlocutors and shows that this definition is incompatible with other beliefs that the same interlocutor holds. For example, in the *Laches*, Laches suggests that courage consists in endurance, but Socrates shows that, while foolish endurance is not courage but rashness, skilled, highly informed practitioners of arts who persevere for the sake of expected results could hardly be called courageous. In contrast, in the transitional *Meno*, Socrates not only asks his well-worn 'what is X?' question (what is virtue?), but also poses some radical challenges to the efficacy of adversarial argument as a means of philosophical discovery, and he even offers a theory of learning as a recollection that already presupposes the immortality of the soul, reincarnation, and a doctrine of innate knowledge. If, for example, the Socratic quest for moral knowledge proceeded through inductive reasoning from examples, as Aristotle suggests, then the idea of innate knowledge seems to part ways with this Socratic idea.

Developmentalism as a way of reading the Platonic dialogues also takes us some way into views about Platonic metaphysics, especially the so-called theory of forms, and internal critiques or modifications by Plato of his earlier work. Because we are studying Socrates, it is not our brief here to engage with these issues. Rather, what is important is that in many of what Vlastos termed the 'middle dialogues,'[5] not only does Socrates continue to be the conversation leader, albeit operating in a much more didactic fashion, but there are also highly detailed biographical reports about Socrates, including, as we saw, in the *Phaedo*, his execution; in the *Symposium*, his initiation into the mysteries of love at the hands of a priestess of the Eleusinian mysteries; and in the *Parmenides*, his encounter with the philosopher Parmenides, who was visiting Athens from Elea and happened to run into the young Socrates. On Vlastos' theory, we are forced to isolate these biographical sketches in the middle dialogues and say that some of them are somehow reflections of the historical Socrates, while also insisting that what Socrates is made to say in these same dialogues, because of its philosophical content, could never be Socratic. This aspect of developmentalism has been, perhaps unglamorously, styled the mouthpiece theory; here Socrates is more or less a cipher who has simply an honorific position in the dialogues and no real philosophical part to play in what are increasingly Plato's own thoughts.[6]

EVALUATING THE DEVELOPMENTALIST APPROACH: THE PROBLEM OF CHRONOLOGY

With this account of Vlastos' Socrates in place, we can ask, first, what evidence does Vlastos offer us that the dialogues' chronology supports developmentalism? What do the data, independently of relying on the dialogues' philosophical content, tell us about the order in which Plato wrote his dialogues. It is almost universally recognized that here, in fact, Vlastos' work is on shaky ground, since his grouping of the dialogues – early Socratic, transitional Socratic–Platonic, middle Platonic and late Platonic – is not supported by statistical or stylistic analyses of Plato's text.[7]

The dating of Plato's dialogues has been a scholarly obsession for over a century, and most of the work of the pioneers, such as Lewis Campbell and Dittenberger, the founder of stylometry, has withstood the test of time. Primarily, these scholars have succeeded in isolating a late group of Plato's dialogues on the basis of the remarkably consistent use of certain linguistic practices, including the avoidance of vowel hiatus between two Greek words, the use of technical philosophical vocabulary and the presence of particles of speech. What their results show is that most of Plato's dialogues belong in a large group that includes both aporetic dialogues and the great dramatic dialogues that adumbrate and develop Plato's metaphysics, as well as offer vivid portraits of Socrates. Thus, whereas Vlastos' early, Socratic dialogues excluded both the *Symposium* and the *Phaedo* precisely on philosophical grounds, stylistically there is no difference between these dialogues and such dialogues as the *Apology*, *Crito* or *Euthyphro*. The upshot is that the developmental hypothesis is not supported by a chronology of Plato's writings.[8]

PLATO'S SOCRATES: AN EXEMPLARY PHILOSOPHICAL LIFE

What, then, are we to make of the character Socrates whom we find in Plato's dialogues? To begin to answer this question, we must see that Plato sets his dialogues in the heyday of the great Sophists, at the height of Periclean Athens, with Socrates in his prime. In reality, Plato wrote the dialogues after the defeat of Athens in the war with Sparta, when people such as Protagoras, Gorgias, Hippias and even Parmenides no longer visited Athens, and the Sophists were instead represented by Isocrates and his school. Socrates' followers had gone their own separate ways, and Plato was already engaging his own philosophical community, which in time became a formally recognized institution, Plato's Academy. As his writing probably occupied the years between 383 and 366 BCE, Plato cast his gaze backwards into the fifth century BCE, conveying an intellectual and broader cultural world at the centre of which he placed Socrates. His portrait of Socrates interweaves several tasks: Plato recognizes Socrates as an exemplary human being, references Socratic philosophical commitments and inquires into the philosophical genealogy of Socrates. All of these researches inform Plato's work; at times they compete with each other or even cancel each other out to create a labyrinth of misdirection.

We have already seen (chapter one) some traces of the exemplary portrayal of Socrates in the birth of the Socratic literature of the fourth century BCE. For his part, Plato likens Socrates to Theseus entering the labyrinth (*Phaedo*), to Orpheus descending into the underworld (*Symposium*), to Odysseus in search of his comrades (*Protagoras*) and to Zalmoxis returning from the dead (*Charmides*). Within these narrative frames, Socrates takes on the role of the traditional Greek hero, dedicated to his mission (*Apology*), obedient to a higher authority (*Apology*) and acting for the salvation of his community. Most often in Plato this activity takes the form of a spiritual combat, with Socrates fighting against people who, one might assume, owing to the high reputation they enjoyed, would exemplify certain virtues. Usually these conversations are punctuated by exchanges with younger men, some ambitiously set on positions of honour in Athens, others evidently well-bred youths who typify perhaps more conventional views worthy of scrutiny, and others still Socratics in their own right, people who might be expected to have some familiarity with Socratic discourse. In contrast, Xenophon's *Memorabilia* tends to focus attention more directly on the question of who was and who was not a member of Socrates' inner circle, if such there was, and to allow a greater social variety of conversational partners: Socrates and a courtesan named Theodote reveal secrets in the art of seduction, for example, as we saw in the previous chapter. In addition, some of the titles of the missing Socratic dialogues – *Simon*, *Aspasia*, *Zopyrus* – show Socrates conversing with women, working-class people or shopkeepers, and foreigners. Even in the more polite society of the Platonic dialogues, however, Socrates talks to a very wide range of people. As Nails has written: 'the first person to speak in *Republic* I is a slave; Cephalus is an immigrant, and his is a family of *metics* several of whose female members we know to have been alive (i.e., as in *Symposium*, women are also in the house); Thrasymachus is a foreign visitor; Charmantides is visiting from a rural deme, is of the highest class, and has inherited wealth; Niceratus represents "new money" (i.e., Nicias had become wealthy through mining); Adeimantus and Glaucon are from an urban deme and are further down the class ranks; Socrates is poor; Clitophon is noteworthy primarily as a political flip-flop.'[9]

Plato narrates Socrates' intervention in what we might call business as usual in Athens, in his critique of the values of *pleonexia,* or greed, both on a social and on a personal scale, partially, as we have seen, in terms of an exemplary tradition. But he also reflects on the philosophical exploits of Socrates in their own right, placing him alongside social and ethical theorists within a philosophical lineage of varying hue. Plato also shows us that the power of Socrates' moral critique is due to the force of a uniquely Socratic forum for philosophical investigation: the elenchus. Were there Socratic doctrines, theses, teachings, and did these together constitute a philosophy of Socrates? The answer to this question is, like everything Socratic, fraught with difficulties.

SOCRATES' APORETIC PERSONA

As we have seen, all of the dialogues that Vlastos considered 'Socratic' are aporetic: they take the form of conversations pursued with a number of interlocutors whose views are elicited, shown to entail contradictions and dismissed. These dialogues end in impasse and are destructive, showing only that the virtue in question has not been successfully defined. The Greek word for this process of interrogation or examination of the interlocutor is *elenchus* – a word that has the primary meaning in Classical Attic of 'refutation',[10] or even 'to impugn the honor of'.[11] Thus we can readily see how a method such as this would be effective in criticizing someone's beliefs; it is harder to see how the mere refutation of poorly thought-through opinions (the Greek word for 'opinion' is *doxa*, and in Plato, *doxa* almost invariably has a negative connotation) will result in the discovery of truths, or even moral improvement, given the humiliating effect of being subject to refutation in a public setting. Indeed, many of Socrates' 'patients' seemed unmoved by their encounters with Socrates, or, on the contrary, positively enraged at Socrates:

> While we were speaking, Thrasymachus had tried many times to take over the discussion but was restrained by those sitting near him, who wanted to hear our argument to the end. When we paused after what I'd just said, however, he couldn't keep quiet any longer. He coiled himself up like a wild beast about to spring, and he hurled himself at us as if to tear us to pieces. (R 3369a)

In the *Apology*, Socrates links his 'mission' from Apollo with this unique method:

> He [Chaerephon] went to Delphi at one time and ventured to ask the oracle – as I say gentlemen, do not create a disturbance – he asked if any man was wiser than I, and the Pythian replied that no one was wiser . . .
> When I heard of this reply I asked myself: whatever does the god mean? What is his riddle? I am very conscious that I am not wise at all; what then does he mean by saying that I am the wisest? . . .
> For a long time I was at a loss as to his meaning; then I very reluctantly turned to some such investigation as this; I went to one of those reputed wise, thinking that there, if anywhere, I could refute the oracle and say to it, This man is wiser that I, but you said I was. Then, when I examined this man . . . my experience was something like this:
> I thought that he appeared wise to many people and especially to himself, but he was not. I then tried to show him that he thought himself wise, but that he was not. As a result he came to dislike me, and so did many of the bystanders. (21a–d1, with omissions)

The confession of ignorance that Socrates clearly makes in this story matches the negative results of the elenctic dialogues: we only discover what is not courage (*Laches*), not temperance (*Charmides*), not piety (*Euthyphro*) and not justice (*Republic* I). How might these dismal results square with Socrates' illustrious reputation as the founder of Western philosophy? How, more modestly, might Socrates be shown to be practising philosophy at all? Perhaps Socrates is really just arguing *ad hominem* in these encounters; his purpose really is the examination of lives, not of arguments, as one of Socrates' interlocutors proclaims in the *Laches*:

> Whoever comes into close contact with Socrates and associates with him in conversation must necessarily, even if he began by conversing about something quite different in the first place, keep on being led about by the man's arguments until he submits to answering questions about himself concerning both his present manner of life and the life he has lived hitherto. (187e4–9)

So far our preview of Socrates in Plato's dialogues has concentrated on the elenctic or aporetic dialogues, the generally short sketches where Socrates carries out the examination, the elenchus, he outlines in the *Apology*. Socrates does not shrink from calling himself a benefactor of the city for this very reason, that in these examinations he exhorts his fellow citizens to a life of virtue. In the *Apology* Socrates says that he approaches each citizen 'like a father or elder brother, exhorting you to regard virtue' (31b). His primary device for delivering this exhortation is the elenchus, and it is primarily in his guise as a divinely sent gadfly (*Ap.* 30e) that his interlocutors come in for such rough treatment. Reading the stories of their defeat provides the audience with an entertainment that seems to be at the expense of the complacent interlocutor.

Sometimes, indeed, it seems that Socrates will stop at nothing to diminish his interlocutor's standing, while refusing to contribute anything positive to the conversation of his own. How is it that Socrates can get away with this odd mixture of overweening confidence, and what seems an almost unbelievable disavowal of wisdom? How sincere are Socrates' dealings in the elenctic dialogues, and what is the tenor of his conduct? Thrasymachus makes us wonder along with him in the *Republic*:

> By Heracles, he said, that's just Socrates' usual irony. I knew, and I said so to these people earlier, that you'd be unwilling to answer and that, if someone questioned you, you'd be ironical and do anything rather than give an answer. (337a)

SOCRATIC IRONY (AND SINCERITY) IN PLATO

One of the signature traits of Plato's Socrates is precisely his characteristic irony, and it is this quality that many have seized upon as
conveying to us something of the 'real' Socrates. The works of Gregory
Vlastos (*Socrates, Ironist and Moral Philosopher*[12]) and Alexander
Nehamas (*The Art of Living*[13]) present us with a Socratic philosophy
that is thoroughly rooted in irony. For Vlastos, Socratic irony is relatively benign, bereft as it must be of any hint of deceit: Socrates speaks
the truth by saying the opposite of what he means. Here, Vlastos suggests that Socrates is more than just a destructive force for the good,
we might say. Rather, concealed in the familiar arsenal of questions,
assent to which Socrates inevitably secures, that is in the premises
from which Socrates is able to elicit a contradiction of the interlocutor's thesis, is a compromise wisdom, human wisdom, as Socrates
calls it in the *Apology*. Socrates does not have scientific knowledge or
expert political knowledge adequate for giving advice on policy to his
fellow citizens; nevertheless, he has a kind of knowledge derived
empirically from years of sifting the souls of his fellow human beings.
It is this, what Vlastos calls elenctically supported knowledge, which
is the hidden engine of the Socratic conversation.[14]

In this sense, Socratic irony conceals the seeds of an ethical theory,
or at least a set of ethical theses. Sometimes these theses are thought
to be deployed in the Socratic dialogues in the form of the so-called
Socratic paradoxes – namely, that no one does wrong voluntarily, that
virtue is knowledge, and so forth. We shall return to the topic of
Socratic ethics in chapter six. For Nehamas, on the contrary, Socratic
irony is not transparent, but a complex amalgam of openness and
concealment designed to avoid detection by any who do not merit the
discernment of the real meaning of one's words. Nehamas' approach
to Socratic irony is less entertaining for us, the readers; we are inexo-
rably drawn into the fire of Socratic criticism, according to him,
because Socrates' speech has two audiences – the one intended to
understand the meaning and the other not intended to understand the
meaning. For Nehamas, Socrates did not have a moral system. Plato
tried to give us a version of Socrates in his dialogues, and through
them he tried to capture some of the main features of Socrates' inimitable life. Plato, by imitating Socratic irony, allows the reader to
participate in Socrates' original irony, for the reader feels superior to
Plato's characters, even though he may neglect his own virtue. In this
sense, Socratic irony works at the expense of its readers.

THE OBJECTIVES OF PLATO'S SOCRATES

To leave the discussion of Plato's Socrates at this juncture would be to leave intact an impression that Socrates is primarily a moral philosopher; this could well turn out to be the case (recall that Aristotle says: 'Socrates, however, was occupying himself with the moral virtues, having been the first to search for universal definitions of them'; *Meta.* 1078b17). Could it be that Xenophon and Plato agree that Socrates is really more like a moral reformer, or preceptor, and less like a philosopher? Notice that Aristotle in the sentence quoted here says that Socrates was concerned with moral virtues, but that he was so because he was pursuing another subject, namely universal definition of moral terms. Indeed, Plato's Socrates is not just the fiery preacher whom we encounter in the *Apology*; he is also and perhaps above all a seeker of wisdom. In the story about Apollo's oracle, it was Socrates' interrogation of the meaning of the oracle, and in particular of the wisdom it referenced, that instigated the elenchus. How, indeed, could Socrates avoid the study of its wisdom in its own right and merely rest content with Xenophon's 'helpfulness' when for him 'virtue is knowledge of the good' How are people to acquire this knowledge, and what is the good, to begin with, other than conformity to the norms of decency embodied, for example, in Xenophon's *kalokagathia*? Socrates' reputation as a philosopher rather rests on statements in the *Apology* such as 'The unexamined life is not worth living' (38a5–6). Indeed, how quickly Socrates turns from tiresome moralist to radical elitist: does Socrates mean to suggest that almost everyone, no matter how well behaved they are, no matter how 'moral', and hence not particularly in need of instruction in this arena, and no matter how 'immoral', is leading a worthless life if he or she is not, in Socrates terms, a philosopher? Does the Socratic examination alone confer value on a life that would otherwise be bereft of meaning?[15] Socrates acknowledges the shock value of his proclamation when he says: 'If I say that this is the greatest good for a human being – to have discussions every day about virtue and the other things about which you hear me conversing and examining myself and others – and that the unexamined life is not worth living for a human being, you will be still less persuaded by what I say' (38a1–6).

The call to an examined life is connected to a Socratic conception of the good that we do not see as clearly articulated in the non-Platonic

Socratic literature. There, in contrast, we do not find a Socrates who also says that the greatest good for a human being is 'to have discussions every day about virtue' (*Ap.* 38a3) and other ethical matters.

Elsewhere in the Socratic dialogues, Socrates repeats that he is benefiting his fellow citizens, exposing their ignorance, not merely to embarrass them into decency but, seemingly, to turn them into philosophers, into lovers of wisdom:

> So too now I say that this is what I am doing, investigating the argument on my own behalf, certainly, but *equally* as well on behalf of my other companions; or do you not think that it is a *common good* among virtually all human beings, for each thing to be completely evident, as to what it is in reality? (*Ch.* 166d4)

What is this truth that is the object of such ardent pursuit, and why should Socrates say, as he does, for example, in the *Euthydemus*: 'What then is the consequence of what has been said? Is it anything other than that of all the other things, none is either good or bad, but as to these two things, wisdom is good, ignorance bad?' (281e4–5).

Here again we see the paradigmatic aspect of Plato's project – evinced above in the qualities of divine and civic service – coming to take a more pointed form as a recommendation to lead a life of philosophy, even to live for the sake of wisdom, if, as Socrates implies in the quote from the *Euthydemus* above, wisdom is the good. Of course, we will want to know, why is wisdom good? Why is the philosophical life the recommended life?

Plato's Socrates apparently gets into trouble with his fellow citizens not only for making this assumption but for actually making them an offer they cannot well refuse, for he seems to insist that they all live this examined life along with him: 'Meletus being vexed on behalf of the poets, Anytus on behalf of the craftsmen and politicians' (*Ap.* 23e4). If, then, this wisdom alone is what allows human beings to lead lives worthy of them, the implication is that all human beings are capable of becoming philosophers, as we saw above in the quotation from the *Charmides*, and as we see again in what Socrates has to say about virtue in the *Meno*, where Socrates explicitly says: 'so all human beings are good in the same way, for they become good by acquiring the same qualities. . . . Then the virtue of all is the same' (73c1–8).

THE VARIOUS STANCES OF THE PLATONIC 'SOCRATES'

We have covered a lot of territory in this preliminary survey of Plato's Socrates. Before concluding this overview of some of the features of the aporetic dialogues and the philosophical commitments, or at least interest, of Socrates that they perhaps reveal (to the extent that they may or may not be reflections of the historical Socrates), we return again to the developmental hypothesis, and in particular to the merits of isolating these dialogues as more genuinely Socratic.

Consider the Socratic assumption that the common good for all human beings is to know the truth or even that all human beings should embrace the life of philosophy (what exactly this will turn out to be we have not yet said). Here, if anywhere, we owe it to Socrates to defend him against charges of political elitism of the kind that, as we saw above, he perhaps attracted. The language of *Apology* 20a–b, when Socrates recounts the advice he gave to his wealthy companion Callias ('Callias, I said, if your two sons had been colts or calves, we should have had no difficulty in finding and engaging a trainer') now begins to take on a different overtone. Socrates never found such an expert; for this very reason, he regarded it as the human imperative to pursue wisdom. In contrast, the Socrates whom we find in the later books of the *Republic*, especially books III and following, seems to deny that all, most or even many human beings share in this philosophical imperative. Instead, almost everyone by nature lacks the capacity to be a philosopher.

Plato fabricates a society and, with it, a mythology that define all individuals in terms of static types, as people in whom certain kinds of desire dominate: gold, lovers of wisdom; silver, lovers of honour; and bronze, lovers of bodily appetites and of wealth. Now, not only is there a sharp distinction, possibly even a genetic distinction, between philosophers and non-philosophers, but only the former, philosophers, can be genuinely happy, because only they by nature are capable of undertaking the most arduous study – the study of what Plato calls the Form of the Good.

What of the rest of society? The silver and bronze non-philosophers will be trained by their intellectual superiors to follow the prescriptions handed down to them for happiness; their agency, such as it is, is manipulated through emotional, preconscious or pre-rational methods. Glaring differences between dialogues such as the *Apology* and the *Republic* make the developmental hypothesis more compelling.

Other differences among the aporetic dialogues, particularly over the question of knowledge itself, are equally stark. In the *Laches*, Socrates asks Laches, expressing some impatience with the previous examples, to define courage: 'what is that common quality, which is the same in all these cases, and which is called courage?' And again: 'what is that common quality which is called courage, and which includes all the various uses of the term when applied both to pleasure and pain, and in all the cases to which I was just now referring?' (192b–e). Here we see what justifies Aristotle's ascription to Socrates of an interest in universal definition; nevertheless, at the end of the dialogue Socrates forces his interlocutors to admit: 'then, Nicias, we have not discovered what courage is.' The pattern displayed here is consistent with several other aporetic dialogues (that's why we call them aporetic: they end in irresolution).

Now, when we meet Socrates in the *Phaedo*, suddenly things seem very different. Socrates refers to 'knowledge of absolute equality'. Even more astonishing, at *Phaedo* 100b–c, Socrates says he is going to expound his own theory of causation and, further, that he is going to start from a principle that his hearers have already become very familiar with; not only that, but he is going to 'assume the existence of absolute beauty and goodness and magnitude and all the rest of them'.

Out of the blue, apparently, Socrates in this dialogue is represented as having long held a theory of causation, assuming the existence of absolute essences, and as having made his listeners long since familiar with all of this, whereas the *aporia* of the elenctic dialogues would argue that here, in the *Phaedo*, Socrates must be out of his mind! When have we heard of anything absolute? How, if Socrates has no wisdom, great or small, can he possibly have a theory of causation that he is able to explain to others? Again, perhaps even more perplexing is the conversation that the youthful Socrates (Plato makes the narrator say, 'Socrates was then quite young') has with the famous philosopher Parmenides of Elea. Parmenides asks Socrates:

> Tell me. Have you yourself distinguished as separate, in the way you mention, certain forms themselves, and also as separate the things that partake of them? And do you think that likeness itself is something, separate from the likeness we have? (130b2–5)

It is in passages such as the one from the *Phaedo* and the one from the *Parmenides* that, some would say, we see proof positive of developmentalism. How can the Socrates who in the *Apology* just takes up the life of philosophy on the assumption that he has no wisdom be the same Socrates who, at the age of 20, say, expounds the theory of forms with total conviction to the greatest philosopher of his age? According to Vlastos, to explain this radical *volte-face*, we must suppose that 'when [Socrates] discards the elenchus as the right method to search for the truth, it is because Plato has now lost faith in that method himself' (Vlastos 1988, 373). Yet other scholars[16] would say that what we have here is actually an indication that Plato has prepared us, his readers, for the full-blown metaphysical theory of essential qualities that we see in the *Phaedo* by anticipating them and giving grounds for their existence in the aporetic dialogues. Recall that Socrates asks for the 'common quality of courage that is the same in all cases'. How on earth could he demand this kind of definition or even assume that there is such a quality answering to the question unless he already believed in the forms, essential properties?

If we prefer to view the relationship between the aporetic and constructive dialogues[17] in this way, with the former anticipating themes in the latter, we might then endorse a proleptic reading of the dialogues. This is a highly persuasive way of reading the Socratic dialogues, that is as fully Platonic in the sense that they prepare the ground for philosophical themes that Plato has always been interested in, and they do so by asking preliminary questions concerning philosophical theses that Plato expounds and sometimes appears committed to. Nonetheless, if we adopt the proleptic approach, we still must keep in mind that *someone* died in 399 BCE, and that this person, whose life is dramatized in the works of Plato and other Socratics, was a philosopher, not a cipher.

The reader should always keep in mind, however, that in contrasting the aporetic Socrates with the chock-full-of-knowledge variety, brimming with confidence, expounding theories to which he is fully committed and whose veracity he could scarcely doubt, we should not thereby make the mistake of thinking that Plato himself was fully dogmatic in this sense. There are plenty of passages in which those very confidently expressed theories seem to fade away in the wake of massive problems, and this is true in every field of Platonic philosophy, from metaphysics to psychology to politics. Aporetic philosophy as a problem-based approach to studying does not go away 'after' the Socratic dialogues.

FURTHER READING

Benson, H. (ed.) 1992. *Essays on the Philosophy of Socrates*. Oxford: Oxford University Press.

Blondell, R. 2002. *The Play of Character in Plato's Dialogues*. Cambridge: Cambridge University Press. This is a good resource on the character of 'Socrates' in the dialogues, as are the following four sources.

Brickhouse, T. and Smith, N. 1994. *Plato's Socrates*. Oxford: Oxford University Press.

Rowe, C. 2007. 'The form of the good and the good in Plato's *Republic*', in Cairns, D., Herrmann, F. and Penner, T. eds. *Pursuing the Good: Ethics and Metaphysics in Plato's Republic*. Edinburgh: Edinburgh University Press, 124–53. A highly non-developmentalist account.

Vlastos, G. 1991. *Socrates, Ironist and Moral Philosopher*. Ithaca, NY: Cornell University Press.

—. 1994. *Socratic Studies*. Ed. M. Burnyeat. Oxford: Oxford University Press.

CHAPTER FIVE

SOCRATIC METHOD AND EPISTEMOLOGY

THE ELENCHUS

In addition to works written by Plato himself and reflecting, as we have seen, the philosophy and life of Socrates, we possess what are called the pseudo-platonic dialogues, which were written by close associates studying with Plato, who no doubt continued to think about issues he initially raised. One such dialogue is the *Clitophon*, a very short piece that is apparently a summary of Socratic philosophy written by an academic. The dialogue is couched as a complaint about Socrates as a teacher of virtue:

> I finally got tired of begging for an answer. I came to the conclusion that while you're better than anyone at turning a man towards the pursuit of virtue . . . there are only two possibilities, either you don't know [sc. what virtue is] or you don't wish to share it with me.
>
> For I will say this, Socrates, that while you're worth the world to someone who hasn't yet been converted to the pursuit of virtue, to someone who's already been converted you rather get in the way of his attaining happiness by reaching the goal of virtue. (410b–e with omissions)

Of interest for us is how this pseudo-Platonic dialogue is already able to interrogate the philosophy of Socrates in ways that are still pursued today: the *Clitophon* seems to ask, is Socrates just a philosopher for beginners, and why does he refuse to share his knowledge of virtue with others, if indeed he has any? If he has no knowledge of virtue, then what does his philosophical inquiry seek to accomplish?

We shall study these questions and complaints in the next two chapters, looking first more closely at Socratic method and then at what, if anything, Socratic ethics has to teach us.

As we saw, the Socratic dialogues tend to converge around a single practice, the Socratic examination, interview, elenchus, conversation. Whichever word we use – and Plato uses all of these words[1] – the dialogue's drama unfolds as a search for a definition, accompanied by a refutation of candidates offered for the definition. Often the interlocutor receives a lesson from Socrates in the task of producing well-formed definitions; for example, the definition might initially fail simply because it is not universal enough, as in this example from the *Laches*:

> SOCRATES: As I might ask what is the property which is called Quickness and which is found in running, in playing the lyre, in speaking, in learning, and in many other similar actions, or rather which we possess in nearly every type of action that is worth mentioning of arms, legs, mouth, voice, mind – would you not apply the term 'quickness' to all of them?
>
> LACHES: Quite true.
>
> SOCRATES: And if I were to be asked by someone, What is this thing, Socrates, which, in all of these activities, you call Quickness? I would say that Quickness is that which accomplishes much in little time – whether in running or in any other sort of action.
>
> LACHES: And you would be speaking rightly.
>
> SOCRATES: And now, Laches, try to tell me in like manner what Courage is. (192a–b)

Inevitably, however, the definition will 'fail' in the sense that it will be shown to be inconsistent with one or more premises elicited from the interlocutor. Moreover, it is not just definitions that are the object of refutation; methods, persons, lives – all of these are subject to refutation. We shall discuss the object of refutation and the *ad hominem* character many see in it below.

ELENCHUS IN ACTION: THE *EUTHYPHRO*

For now, it is enough to see that in the dialogues of definition, the engine driving the entire dialogue is Socrates asking his interlocutor

the 'what is X?' question: for example, 'what is piety?' (*Euth.* 5c–d);
'what is justice?' (*R* I); 'what is courage?' (*La.* 190d); 'what is friendship?' (*Ly.* 223b7–8); 'what is the fine?' (*Hi. Mi.*); 'what is self-control?'
(*Ch.*); 'what is love?' (*Symp.*). Although these elenctic interludes
create the primary momentum of the dialogue, they are themselves
sometimes motivated questions that arise from life and how best to
live it. So, for example, in the *Laches*, two generals are concerned
about the education of their sons. Specifically, they want to know
whether the highly technical art of learning how to master solo
combat in heavy armor will help their sons to succeed as citizen-
soldiers. Socrates demurs on the question at hand and instead guides
the generals to the question posed at 190c, 'what is courage?' In a
similar way, Euthyphro is on his way to register a charge of homicide
against his own father. The older man had a slave – himself accused
of murdering another slave – thrown into a ditch while the master
consulted the oracle about how to treat the slave he was accusing. In
the meantime, the accused man has died in custody, and Euthyphro
has set about accusing his own father of murder to avoid the stain of
blood pollution, which, under Athenian law, accrued to the one who
sheltered a murderer. Obviously, many of the players in this story are
acting on their beliefs about what is sanctioned by religion. The father
consults the oracle, but meanwhile his slave dies. The son is prosecuting his father for homicide, but in the process violates the sanction
against parricide. Moreover, he is having his father indicted at the same
court and on the same day that Socrates himself receives the *graphe
paranomon*, the indictment for atheism (cf. chapter two). The question
that Socrates poses at 5c8, 'by Zeus, tell me what you just now affirmed
you clearly know; what sort of thing do you say the pious and the
impious are?', is also expected by the fact that Euthyphro himself is
posing as an expert in prophesying and as a religious authority.

The background issues, then, to Socrates posing his 'what is it?'
question pertain to matters of expertise, authority and the possibility,
or lack thereof, of human certainty in the face of matters of life and
death. Nevertheless, the way that Socrates asks the question at 5c6–e7
seems to land us far afield from anything that could solve life's problems, whether extraordinary or ordinary. Socrates asks Euthyphro:

Isn't the pious the same as itself in every action, and the impious,
again, the contrary of the pious in its entirety, but like itself and

everything whatever that is to be impious, having, with respect to its impiety, some one idea?

[Euthyphro answers as follows]
Piety is prosecuting one who commits injustice, whether it is about murders or temple robberies, or does wrong in any other such way, whether it is actually one's father or mother or anyone else, and not prosecuting is impious. (5d9 ff.)
[Socrates responds to Euthyphro and rejects the definition offered]
But, Euthyphro, many other things you would say are pious as well. (6d6–8)

What is wrong with Euthyphro's answer, and what does this tell us about the kind of answer Socrates is looking for?

Euthyphro says that any time someone prosecutes another who has committed an injustice, this is an instance of piety. And his reason for saying so is to show that he, Euthyphro, is doing something pious by prosecuting his father, even though most Greeks would consider it to be the summit of impiety to take legal action against one's own father.

Now, commentators often say that Euthyphro's answer is formally wrong because for example, it does not satisfy requirements for completeness or for substitutability: not all instances of prosecuting someone for impiety are pious, and not all pious actions consist in prosecuting someone for impiety. True enough, but here the answer is also materially wrong: the great irony in this dialogue is that those who are prosecuting Socrates for impiety are most grievously impious, as we, the readers, are supposed to understand. Socrates tries to give Euthyphro some help at this point, and so he sets out some criteria for definition: 'remember that I did not ask you to teach me one or two of the many holy things, but this form itself by which all the holy things are holy' (6d9–11). Similarly, Laches follows up his rejected answer, 'if someone remaining in the ranks is willing to face the enemy and not flee, know well that he is courageous' (a.190e4–6), with another attempt: 'it seems to me now that courage is an endurance of the soul, if it is necessary to mention the thing which is essential in all these cases' (192b9–c1). Socrates insists that there is an essential idea or form that makes pious things pious and brave actions brave. Moreover, he claims that pious things are pious *because of* this essential form. When Euthyphro, on his second attempt to define piety, suggests that it is 'what is loved by all the gods', he gives what he takes to be the essence of piety and tries to give an answer that satisfies the completeness requirement: all pious actions are loved by the gods, and whatever action is loved by the gods is a pious action. Why is Socrates still not happy with the answer? When I was growing up, there was a television commercial that featured a character called Charlie the Tuna. This fish was always looking for a way to be caught and sold under the brand Starkist Tuna. Why? Charlie reasons that, since all Starkist Tuna taste good, if he becomes a Starkist Tuna, he too will taste good. In the commercial we are told, 'only good tasting tuna get to be Starkist'. Here, then, we have Euthyphro's problem: something is not pious *because* the gods love it; rather the gods love it because it is pious. We have not yet identified the essential causal feature that brings about or, we could say, gives a reason why the gods love what is pious.

THE 'SOCRATIC FALLACY'

One objection to Socrates' brand of intellectualism is that the search for a definition of virtue involves what is called honorifically the 'Socratic fallacy'. Consider, for example, the *Euthyphro*: Euthyphro justifies his prosecution of his own father by appealing to a definition of piety that will automatically include this particular action under the rubric of piety, which is identical to prosecuting those accused of religious crimes. So Socrates wants Euthyphro to appeal to a definition of piety in order to understand whether this particular act is pious. Putting the story this way makes it seem as if Socrates needs to know the definition of something before he can know anything about it. Will fighting in armour make one brave? Well, let's see: first we have to define courage.

The *Meno* opens with Meno asking about the Sophistic thesis, whether virtue can be taught. In response, Socrates pretends to be an imaginary Athenian and says that he doesn't know whether virtue can be taught because he does not know 'in any way at all what virtue is' (71a5–7). He then compares his dilemma to that of someone who asks a question about the person Meno but has no idea at all about Meno, having never met him. How could that person be in any way a reliable informant about any aspect of Meno?

You must think I am someone blessed by the gods to know whether Virtue can be taught or how it is attained. In truth, I am far from knowing whether or not it can be taught – indeed, I do not happen to know what Virtue, itself, is. . . . How can I know what sort of thing something is when I do not even know what it is? Do you suppose that somebody who does not in any way know who Meno is could know whether he was noble or rich or well-born or the reverse? Is that possible, do you think? (71a–b)

In a similar way, Socrates, it is often claimed, relies on a principle that has been called the priority of definition. According to this principle, we cannot know anything about a given virtue unless we first know the definition of that virtue.[2]

Another example may be found in the *Euthyphro*:

SOCRATES: By Zeus, Euthyphro! Do you think that you have such accurate knowledge of divine things and what is pious and impious that in circumstances like you describe, you can accuse your own father? Are you not, yourself, afraid that you are committing an impious act? (4e3)

Nowhere in the texts does Socrates expressly espouse this principle. However, various passages show that Socrates at least considers it difficult to recognize certain cases that are adduced as examples of something with a highly contentious definition. Indeed, the so-called Socratic fallacy generalizes this difficulty and states that for Socrates 'it is impossible to search for a definition F by means of examples of things that are F'.[3]

Consider the following text:

SOCRATES: If you did not know precisely what is pious and impious, it is unthinkable that . . . you would ever be moved to prosecute your venerable father. (*Eu.* 15d)

As this book is not centrally about Plato, but about Socrates, we shall need to pause, but only for a brief discussion of the language that Socrates uses in the *Euthyphro* as well as in the *Laches*, pointing out, first, that certain words in both passages, namely, *eidos* ('form'), *idea* ('idea'), *ousia* ('essence') and *aition* ('cause'), are all part of the vocabulary associated with the theory of forms: the metaphysics of essence

SOCRATES: A GUIDE FOR THE PERPLEXED

that asserts that there are real, essential properties that give particulars their characteristics and allow them to be predicated correctly with the relevant property. There is almost no difference between what Socrates says in the *Phaedo* about the Form of the Equal and the criteria for definition that he develops for Euthyphro concerning piety.

In the *Phaedo*, Socrates says that 'all beautiful things are beautiful by the Beautiful' (100d3). Similarly, as we saw in the *Euthyphro*, Socrates demands from Euthyphro that he state the form itself that makes all pious actions pious.

The upshot for the discussion so far is this: insofar as we are looking for something distinctively Socratic in the dialogues of definition, we have not really found it in the definitions for which Socrates is constantly in search. Insofar as he is after a unique form that is 'a model' by which to determine which actions are and are not pious, he apparently presupposes this very thing, a form that accounts for the pious. And this assumption, in turn, seems incompatible with the disavowal of knowledge, with a metaphysically or epistemologically naive Socrates, and so with the specifications that, we saw, were associated with Vlastos' Socrates. What we have found in the search for definitions in the early dialogues is actually in conformity with what Aristotle says in the *Metaphysics*: Socrates was looking for the definitions of moral terms and 'he did not separate the forms'. In these so-called Socratic dialogues, Plato uses the very words that he uses regularly in the *Republic* and *Phaedo*, envisioning the object of definition – piety, temperance or courage – as an *eidos*, *ousia* and *idea*.

If we are to search for the Socratic in the dialogues of definition, we need to look again at the examples of Socratic elenchus and at the list of rejected answers:

- Courage is standing in line at the battlefield.
- Justice is returning pledges.
- Temperance is doing things quietly.
- Piety is prosecuting injustice.
- Justice is what is in other people's interest.

All of these formulations posit the virtue in question as belonging to actions. In contrast, for Socrates, it is people who are virtuous; specifically their souls are virtuous, not actions. The same action can be both just and unjust, pious and impious, courageous and uncourageous. But what makes the action virtuous is the state of the soul, the inner disposition, of the person who is acting. The answers that Socrates' interlocutors try out in their second or third formulations seem to evolve, apparently under pressure from Socrates, into descriptions of inner states: Laches says that courage is wise endurance; Nicias suggests that courage is knowledge of what is to be feared. Again, Critias suggests that temperance is knowledge of knowledge. This emphasis on the inner state of the person reflects what Socrates says in the *Apology*: 'I admonish you not to put wealth or anything else before your souls, how it may be as virtuous as possible.' (3061–2)

THE PURPOSE AND METHOD OF THE ELENCHUS

We have traced the pursuit of definition in the Socratic dialogues and seen that there are various criteria established, some of which have to do with scope, completeness, substitutability and explanatory power, and others of which are more concerned with the object of definition in the first instance: is it an action (we saw that it was not) or a property of a person (yes, and more specifically a state of soul)? Now that these parameters of Socratic definition and, thus, elenchus are in place, we can see why Socrates can expect that those who enjoy a reputation for a virtue would be able to define it, namely, because the definition will turn out to be a description of a state of soul that the subject, the person with the virtue, claims to possess. We can also see why Socrates often says that he is refuting not doctrines, but persons.

We saw above that there is a split in the Socratic dialogues: some of them are dialogues of definition, pursued with relevant experts; others eschew definition, instead testing a variety of Sophistic theses. Thrasymachus (*R* I), Protagoras (*Prot., Th.*), Hippias (*Hi. Mi.*), Gorgias (*Gor.*) and the two notorious practitioners of Eristic, Dionysodorus and Euthydemus (*Euth.*) – all appear in Socratic dialogues that grapple with what we saw above was a loosely unified body of thought concerning the relationship between nature and convention, which also envisaged truth in terms of multiple perspectives, rather than as objective or absolute.[4] Now that we have gone through some examples of definition and of Socrates' theory of definition, it might be a little easier to see the parallels between the questions of Socrates and the disturbing theses of the Sophists. For example, Socrates argues that the same action is both just and unjust, both courageous and cowardly. This very thesis is put forward in the *Dissoi Logoi*, not as support for the idea that there is one unique form of justice, but rather the opposite: there simply is no such things as justice. Connected with their tendency to theorize nature (e.g. the *Protagoras* tells a tale of the origins of human society, Callicles references a state of nature, prior to the triumph of the law, on which the weak rely for protection), the Sophists discussed whether virtue is teachable or whether *arête* is inborn, innate, a matter of natural talent.

The *Dissoi Logoi* discusses what it calls a statement that is 'neither true nor new: it is that wisdom and virtue can neither be taught nor learned'. Now, this question seems to be what is driving many of the elenctic dialogues; it is implicit when Socrates says to Callias, 'if your two sons were colts or calves, we could find a trainer'; it is implicit when Lysimaches is wondering whether he should have his son trained in hoplite combat; and it is implicit when Socrates disputes with Gorgias concerning the practice of rhetoric, whether it is a knack or a genuine art. Socrates gets Gorgias to make the claim that this art teaches virtue. Sometimes Socrates is thought of as having a craft model for virtue. This is a view that is at least as old as Aristotle, who writes as follows in the *Eudemian Ethics*:

> Socrates the elder thought that the end of life was knowledge of virtue, and he used to seek for the definition of justice, courage, and each of the parts of virtue, and this was a reasonable approach, since he thought that all virtues were sciences, and that as soon as one knew [for example] justice, he would be just. Surely as soon as we have learned geometry or house building we are geometers or house builders. That is why he sought the definition of virtue, and not rather how virtue arises or from which conditions. (1261b3 ff.)

There are many passages in Plato's dialogues where Aristotle's acceptance of the craft analogy seems apt. For example, at *Euthydemus* 288d9–291d3, Socrates asks about an art 'that will make him who obtains it happy'.[5] He describes this art on the analogy of productive arts such as generalship and architecture.

This picture of Socratic definition, then, explains to some extent the purpose of the elenchus. On the one hand, if virtue is a kind of knowledge, a *techne*, then perhaps it makes sense to test those who claim to possess it, to see whether they have the requisite knowledge. On the other hand, those who teach an art that pretends to inculcate wisdom and virtue (the Sophists) but in reality caters to human desire, especially to the desire for power, can be refuted simply through the consequences of Sophistic theses and the contradictions they entail. Yet, in the last analysis, Socrates and the Sophists share some fundamentally untraditional views about virtue: surely knowing what the good is, or even the definition of a virtue, does not allow you to claim that virtue or constrain you to do the good. This is the counter-intuitive side of Socrates, and in this sense his pursuit of definition goes against ordinary belief. Most people would not agree that knowing the definition of the good makes you good. Here once more we observe the distinctively Socratic thesis that somehow nevertheless verges dangerously on the Sophistic, in what seems to be a kind of shadow teaching.

Why might Socrates believe that virtue is knowledge, even if he rejects the Sophistic idea, or rather the business strategy, that virtue is teachable (i.e. for the appropriate fee)? We have seen how Socrates can be saved from some of the more uncharitable interpretations that accuse him of ignoring real examples of virtue in favour of an abstract conception that no one, it seems, is able to attain, much less articulate. Socrates does study ordinary human virtue and is concerned with everyday practice. But what does his rigorous demand for definition actually add to human life? If this kind of pursuit is his idea of the 'examined life', what kind of claims can he make for it?

SOCRATES' UNDERLYING PREMISES IN THE ELENCHUS; VLASTOS' 'THE SOCRATIC ELENCHUS'

No doubt a key to these questions is to be found in Socrates' own ignorance. We saw in chapter three that Socrates claims not to know anything fine or good, and that he has no wisdom, great or small. The dialogues of definition pointedly terminate in precisely this admission on the part of Socrates: that he does not know the definition in question. The *Laches* ends with Socrates once again refusing the role of a teacher of virtue:

LYSIMACHUS: What do you say Socrates – will you comply? Are you ready to give assistance in the improvement of the youths?

SOCRATES: Indeed, Lysimachus, I should be very wrong in refusing to aid in the improvement of anybody. And had I shown in this conversation that I had a knowledge which Nicias and

Laches have not, then I admit that you would be right in inviting me to perform this duty, but as we are all in the same perplexity, why should one of us be preferred to another? (200e1–9)

We ought not to consider what people in general will say about us, but rather how we stand with the expert in right and wrong: the one authority who represents the actual truth. If Socrates has been able to do one thing, then, it is to show that there are no experts in the science of being human; there is no one to guarantee our happiness and no one, no matter how high his reputation or how virtuous he happens to be, who can step in when the chips are down and substitute his own judgement for one's own. In the *Meno*, Socrates elaborates this disavowal of knowledge:

> SOCRATES: I share the poverty of my fellow countrymen in this respect and confess to my shame that I have no knowledge about virtue at all.
> MENO: Is this true about yourself, Socrates that you don't even know what virtue is? Is this the report that we are to take home about you?
> SOCRATES: not only that, you may say also that, to the best of my belief, I have never met anyone who did know.
> MENO: What? Didn't you meet Gorgias when he was here?
> SOCRATES: let's leave him out of it, since after all he isn't here. What do you yourself say virtue is? (71b1–d9, with omissions)

Relying on authority will not do; neither will deferral to convention or appeal to common opinion or popular consensus. *Apology* 25a, where Meletus tells us that all members of the polis are capable of improving the young, is an example, for Socrates, of someone taking for granted that what people happen in general to think is just true. And if the Sophist, whose job is persuasion, appeals to what people already happen to think, so much the worse for them.

Socrates' question, why should one of us be preferred to another?, speaks of a radical responsibility that everyone has *vis-à-vis* reality itself, or truth. At *Gorgias* 458a8, Socrates reminds Gorgias of the terms, or, we might say, the contract, on which their continued discourse depends:

I don't suppose there is anything quite so bad for a person as having false belief about the things we're discussing right now. So if you say you're this kind of man, too, let's continue the discussion; but if you think we should drop it, let's be done with it and break it off.

In the previous chapter, we uncovered a puzzle: Socrates claims that his mission consists in exhorting people to follow virtue. But, if virtue can't be defined, what is he exhorting them to do? Is Socrates merely a seeker, or is he a moral teacher? If he is a teacher, then what are his doctrines? In his influential article 'The Socratic elenchus', Vlastos clarified the structure of Socrates' elenctic procedure. In particular, he showed that, in helping the interlocutor to examine his beliefs and, so, to see their inconsistency or limits (perhaps the Socratic adage might be something like 'don't believe everything you think'), Socrates actually used a number of propositions, or theses, over and over again. Apart from the surprising fact that his interlocutors assent to the truth of these elenctic principles even at the expense of their own definitions or simultaneously held views, perhaps the most astonishing thing about the elenctic procedure is, in this sense, its intellectual economy. What makes this agreement so unlikely is, as we have already seen, the very unconventional sound of these state-ments, often called the Socratic paradoxes.

We can study an example of how Socrates deploys the elenctic precepts in the *Charmides*, when Socrates refutes a definition of tem-perance as 'modesty' on the grounds that temperance, since it is a virtue, is always good: 'Temperance, whose presence makes men only good, and not bad, is always good' (161b1). A more powerful example is *Meno* 77b2, where Meno defines virtue as 'desiring fine things and being able to acquire them'. Here Socrates refutes the definition by getting Meno to admit that, after all, no one desires bad things, and hence this desire for the good cannot be (part of) the distinguishing feature of virtue. Likewise, in the exchange below, Socrates begins the elenctic progression from the undisputed premise that everyone desires the good. In the case of the *Gorgias*, he uses the premise to undermine Polus' point that the tyrants have the greatest power in the city.[6]

Then, when we slaughter or banish from the city or deprive of property, we do, they imply, will these acts. But if they are advan-tageous to us, we will them; if harmful, we do not. For as you say, we will the good, not what is neither good nor evil, nor what is evil. If we admit this, then if a man, whether tyrant or rhetorician, kills another or banishes him, and it proves to be to his harm, the man surely does what seems good to him, does he not?

But is he doing what he wills, if his conduct proves harmful? (468)

AN ANALYSIS OF THE PROCEDURE IN THE ELENCHUS

What is needed now is a broader sketch of the elenctic procedure. According to standard analyses of the elenchus, what happens is the following.

Socrates disputes with an interlocutor concerning a particular feature of a virtue (e.g. is virtue teachable?) or a particularly difficult case that may or may not exemplify a given virtue (e.g. Euthyphro's prosecution of his own father). Next, Socrates asks for a definition of the virtue, relying on what some have called the priority of definition (the principle that we cannot know anything about a virtue unless we are able to define it; this has been expressed in a less critical way as the principle that we cannot discern difficult cases unless we have an accurate definition, as we saw in chapter four). After the interlocutor formulates an adequate definition, following the guidelines that demand the essential form, present in all instances of a given virtue, Socrates tests the definition by eliciting agreement to additional premises. It is these premises that appeal to a core number of what we have been calling elenctic principles, though they go by various names in the literature: Socratic paradoxes, elenctic precepts and so on. The rejection of the definition results from the incompatibility of the definition with the additional premises.

Scholars have paid a great deal of attention to the kind of refutation Socrates achieves as a result of the elenchus. Here is Gregory Vlastos' classic schema for elenctic refutation as given in his famous article 'The Socratic elenchcus':

1. The interlocutor, 'saying what he believes', asserts p, which Socrates considers false and targets for refutation.
2. Socrates obtains agreement to further premises, say q and r, which are logically independent of p. The agreement is *ad hoc:* Socrates does not argue for q or for r.

3. Socrates argues, and the interlocutor agrees, that *q* and *r* entail *not-p*.
4. Thereupon Socrates claims that *p* has been proved false, *not-p* true.

Consider, first, the logic of such a refutation. If definition D is not consistent with premises A, B and C, what follows? One, more, or all of them may be false. The logic of the elenchus does not dictate the falsehood of the original definition, yet Socrates and his interlocutors usually behave as if it does. Moreover, Socrates claims that what he is doing is investigating the truth, and even that he has actually 'proved' or 'demonstrated' a thesis just by means of this elenctic refutation. Socrates makes the following claim for this method:

> So too now I say that this is what I am doing, investigating the argument on my own behalf, certainly, but *equally* as well on behalf of my other companions; or do you not think that it is a *common good* among virtually all human beings, for each thing to be completely evident, as to what it is in reality? (*Ch.* 166d4, my italics)

THE IMPASSE AT THE HEART OF THE ELENCTIC PROCEDURE: HOW DOES IT DISCOVER TRUE KNOWLEDGE?

What, then, is the connection between elenctic procedure – the requirement that the interlocutor say what he believes to be true – and the final goal of the elenchus: knowledge of virtue? It would seem that the most it can do is to show that within the context of a certain belief set the thesis must be rejected, not because it is false, but because it is inconsistent with a given interlocutor's other beliefs.[7]

Vlastos' own solution to what he called the problem of the elenchus is to suggest that Socrates has some moral knowledge; that is, he both discovers and transmits a virtue-centred eudaimonism[8] by means of the elenchus. This eudaimonism can be expressed in terms of a number of 'precepts' or 'elenctic principles' that, for Vlastos' Socrates, are always latent members of the interlocutor's belief set. It is because they remain indefeasible in elenctic argument that Socrates can at once endorse the truth of his ethical principles and ironically maintain his disavowal of knowledge.[9] Others have taken Vlastos to task for inventing the problem of the elenchus in the first place. They point out that for his interpretation of the goal of the elenchus, the discovery of an impersonal truth, Vlastos relied too heavily on the latter half of the *Gorgias*.[10] Let us look at the passage that Vlastos makes so much of, especially 508e. Here we find Socrates disputing with Callicles, an arch Sophist, or rather an amplified proponent of some of the central themes of the Sophistic movement, including the strong contrast between *nomos* and *phusis*. For Callicles, the superior human being will satisfy his greatest appetites by depriving the weaker of their property and even freedom; the ordinary human being, unable to practise this form of self-gratification at the expense of others, will falsely praise temperance and seek protection from the stronger in conventions that are designed to check this force of nature.

Socrates replies to this grand programme of theft at the highest level possible, with an invocation of cosmic harmony: Callicles' proposal shows us life out of balance. Socrates concludes the whole discussion with a strong admonition that doing injustice, harming another, is

> at once more shameful and worse for the wrongdoer and for the sufferer. These facts, which were shown to be as I state them some time earlier in our previous discussion, are buckled fast and clamped together by arguments of steel and adamant – at least so it would appear as matters stand. For what I say is always the same – that I know not the truth in these affairs, but I do know that of all whom I have ever met either before or now, no one who put forward another view has failed to appear ridiculous. (508e1–509b1, with omissions)

This passage strongly supports Vlastos' interpretation of the Socratic elenchus: what Socrates lacks is expert, absolute and defining knowledge of virtue. Nevertheless, his experience through a lifetime of testing reveals (in the absence of these strongest criteria for knowledge) what is not yet knowledge, but still justifies his assertion that it is that doing, rather than suffering wrong, that is worse for the one who commits it. What gives Socrates such confidence that he has hit on the truth? Perhaps, as has been suggested,[11] it is the interlocutor's almost pathological advocacy of the opposing thesis. It is because

Socrates is not talking to a yes-man, but rather has advanced to confront a staunch adversary, that Socrates can say:

> So *in reality* (*tôi onti*) your agreement with me already marks the *finishing line of the truth* (*telos . . . tês alêtheias*). (*Gor.* 487e6–7)

These remarks in the *Gorgias* led Vlastos to posit an epistemology underlying the elenchus that explained how Socrates was entitled to claim that he had not only arrived at the truth via this method, but actually succeeded in demonstrating it by means of 'adamantine' arguments, as follows:

> A. Whoever has a false moral belief will always have at the same time true beliefs entailing the negation of that false belief.

> B. The set of elenctically tested moral beliefs held by Socrates at any given time is consistent.

Now, these principles, never openly articulated by Socrates, but suggested by what he says at *Gorgias* 507, would lead us to believe that there are latent beliefs to which Socrates must, again via elenctic examination, gain access. Perhaps more believably, we can say that Socrates here was developing some kind of coherence model of truth. The idea is that false beliefs can be winnowed away: they fit poorly with one's other beliefs, and they also perform poorly, so to speak, in a contest of belief.

FURTHER READING

Benson, H. 2000. *Socratic Wisdom.* Oxford: Oxford University Press. A more detailed treatment of the elenchus.

Beversluis, J. 2000. *Cross Examining Socrates.* Cambridge: Cambridge University Press. A good study of Socrates' treatment of his interlocutors.

Scott, G. (ed.) 2002. *Does Socrates Have a Method?* University Park, PA: Penn State Press. This rehearses some of the issues surrounding the elenchus in a balanced way.

Vlastos, G. 1994. *Socratic Studies.* Ed. M. Burnyeat. Oxford: Oxford University Press. Contains Vlastos' seminal article on the Socratic elenchus.

CHAPTER SIX

HAPPINESS AND VIRTUE

SOCRATIC 'HAPPINESS'

We should not let all of this interest in Socratic method and what may or may not be a Socratic epistemology obscure the content of what Socrates has to say in the elenctic encounters. Although he formulates his premises in a number of ways, most of the propositions that Socrates employs tend to reveal just this intellectualist construal of ethics that we have been exploring in terms of Socratic method. As we have already seen, more than once in the elenctic dialogues Socrates attempts to move his interlocutor away from behavioural descriptions of virtue (bravery is remaining in rank in the hoplite line; temperance is doing things quietly; justice is returning what is owed) to dispositional descriptions (courage is knowledge of the fearful and the hopeful; temperance is knowledge of knowledge). More generally, we have yet to explain why Socrates is after knowledge of virtue in the first place.

In the *Euthydemus*, Socrates' interlocutors are two wisecracking performance artists who specialize in using Sophistic tricks and downright fallacies to trap opponents in a kind of linguistic martial arts. The young Cleinias finds himself an audience member in one of these contests, with Socrates joining as an odd participant, becoming the Sophists' rival for the soul of Cleinias. After a display of verbal wizardry on the part of the two Sophists, Dionysodorus and Euthydemus, Socrates gives a display of his own, showing how he would encourage the youth, Cleinias, to become a philosopher. He begins his 'protreptic'[1] with the somewhat abrupt question:

Do we all wish to do well in the world? Or perhaps this is one of the questions which I feared you might laugh at, for it is foolish, no doubt, even to ask such things. Who in the world does not wish to do well? Not a single one, said Clinias. (278e4)

Socrates is starting with a simple analysis of action: what do we want? The question here is not what should we want, or what would it be right for us to want, but simply what do we in fact want. Here and in other texts, Socrates suggests that what all people want is to be happy. He eventually secures agreement to this premise. Even in the *Meno*, where Meno initially objects that some people want what is bad, Socrates is able to gain Meno's agreement with what we might call the prudential principle – the principle that all wish to be happy, to do well, to enjoy the good:

> SOCRATES: Isn't it clear then that this class, who don't recognize evils for what they are, don't desire evil but what they think is good, though in fact it is evil; those who through ignorance mistake bad things for good obviously desire the good?
>
> MENO: For them I suppose that is true.
>
> SOCRATES: Now as for those whom you speak of as desiring evils in the belief that they do harm to their possessor, these presumably know they will be injured by them?
>
> MENO: They must.
>
> SOCRATES: And don't they believe that whoever is injured is, in so far as he is injured, unhappy?
>
> MENO: That too they must believe.
>
> SOCRATES: And unfortunate?
>
> MENO: Yes.
>
> SOCRATES: Well, does anybody want to be unhappy and unfortunate?
>
> MENO: I suppose not.
>
> SOCRATES: Then if no, nobody desires what is evil, for what else is unhappiness but desiring evil things and getting them. (77e)

Now, looking at these texts, we might ask, what happened to Socratic intellectualism? What happened to Socrates' talk of 'knowing' the

SOCRATES: A GUIDE FOR THE PERPLEXED

good, of finding the definition of virtue, even of loving wisdom, when in the end all we want is to be happy? Does something as ordinary as happiness and the recognition of its place in human life, as the end we all seek, amount to anything like the recommendation for the examined life that, we saw, Socrates seemed willing enough to die for? And what of Socrates' own service to the god, clarifying the meaning of the oracle, or, indeed, his service to his fellow human beings, 'approaching each one like a father or elder brother', caring for their souls and exhorting them to virtue (*Ap*. 31b)? Finally, if all we want is happiness, then why does Socrates insist so strongly that knowing the truth is the common good for all human beings?

To clarify these issues, we return to the *Euthydemus*, where Socrates follows the initial premise that all desire the good, or to be happy, with a question about what the good actually consists in. What about things like health or wealth – things that we might wish to call external goods or even goods of fortune? Will having these things bring us happiness? Socrates answers as follows:

> In sum, I said, it looks like this, Cleinias: as for all the things which at first we said are good, our argument concerning them is not this – that they are by nature good in themselves. Rather this appears to be how things stand; that if ignorance leads them, they are greater bads than their opposites, to the extent that they are more able to serve what leads, it being bad, while if intelligence and wisdom lead, they are greater goods, but in themselves neither of them is worth anything. What then is the consequence of what has been said? Is it anything other than that of all the other things, none is either good or bad, but as to these two things, wisdom is good, ignorance bad? – He agreed. (281d2–e5)

Here Socrates says something very radical: most of the things that human beings acquire in the belief that they are good and will make them happy in themselves are worth nothing: 'all other things [apart from wisdom] are neither good nor bad.' There are a variety of views about what Socrates is getting at when he suggests that wisdom alone is good, while every other thing is neutral. One interpretation suggests that, although Socrates says that wisdom is the only thing good in itself, what Socrates means is that wisdom is the only thing that consistently functions as a means to happiness, to the well-being that, as we saw, Socrates references at the beginning of his conversation with Cleinias. The idea is that Socrates has a view about rational action that he derives from a simple fact that he has noticed about everyone: everyone wants to be happy. Therefore, what a person wants to do when he or she acts is to realize happiness: that is the end of action. Now, knowledge about how things are, combined with knowledge about how to respond to circumstances, will allow a person to act successfully, that is, to act in ways that will most likely improve his or her chances of being happy. This is the kind of wisdom that Socrates is talking about with Cleinias, knowledge that leads to happiness.

Other passages suggest that, for Socrates, it is possible to think about action according to this teleological structure. For example, in the *Lysis*, Socrates is talking to two youths about the topic of friendship: they hold themselves to be each other's friends, but what is the definition of friendship? Here Socrates discusses the structure of desire in terms of a means–end ordering that must culminate in that which is desirable in itself. Thus there are three kinds of things in the world, for the purpose of this analysis: there are good things, things desirable in themselves, intrinsically valuable; bad things, things that no one would want and whose presence is intrinsically harmful; and things that are neither-good-nor-bad (NGNB).[2] Socrates' point is that we 'want' the NGNB for the sake of or on account of what is intrinsically good or desirable:

Soc.: And health is also dear?

Lysis: Certainly.

Soc.: And if dear, then dear for the sake of something?

Lysis: Yes.

Soc.: And surely this object must also be dear, as is implied in our previous admissions?

Lysis: Yes.

Soc.: And that something dear involves something else dear?

Lysis: Yes.

Soc.: But then, proceeding in this way, shall we not arrive at some first principle of friendship or dearness which is not capable of being referred to any other, for the sake of which, as we maintain, all other things are dear, and, having there arrived, we shall stop?

Lysis: True.

Soc.: My fear is that all those other things which, as we say, are dear for the sake of another are illusions and deceptions only, but where that first principle is, there is the true ideal of friendship. Let me put the matter thus: Suppose the case of a great treasure (this may be a son who is more precious to his father than all his other treasures); would not the father, who values his son above all things, value other things also for the sake of his son? I mean, for instance, if he knew that his son had drunk hemlock, and the father thought that wine would save him, he would value the wine?

Lysis: He would.

Soc.: And also the vessel which contains the wine?

Lysis: Certainly.

Soc.: But does he therefore value the three measures of wine, or the earthen vessel which contains them, equally with his son? Is not this rather the true state of the case? All his anxiety has regard not to the means which are provided for the sake of an object, but to the object for the sake of which they are provided. And although we may often say that gold and silver are highly valued by us, that is not the truth, for there is a further object, whatever it may be, which we value most of all, and for the sake of which gold and all out other possessions are acquired by us. Am I not right?

Lysis: Yes, certainly.

Soc.: And may not the same be said of the friend? That which is only dear to us for the sake of something else is improperly said to be dear, but the truly dear is that in which all these so called dear friendships terminate. (220–221d)

For many scholars (see especially Penner and Rowe 2005, 263) this 'truly dear' or 'first friend' must be described either as happiness or as knowledge leading to happiness, in all cases one acts for the sake of the 'first friend', and nothing and no one but this first friend is ever truly or really loved.

THE PRECEPTS OF EUDAIMONIST ETHICS

Most people who read the Socratic dialogues of Plato agree on this point: that Socrates either discovers or endorses a eudaimonist ethics, according to which rational action may be defined as acting in a way that is conducive to one's well-being, or happiness (the Greek word for happiness is *eudaimonia*). Some examples of this interpretation may be seen in the literature. Here is a summary of Irwin's discussion of the structure of Socratic eudaimonism, from his *Plato's Ethics*:

I. (1) In all our rational actions, we pursue our *own* happiness. (2) We pursue happiness only for its own sake, never for the sake of anything else. (3) Whatever else we additionally pursue we pursue it for the sake of happiness.

II. The remarks in the *Euthydemus* about happiness, taken by themselves, imply only that if we do not pursue our *own* happiness, we are not acting rationally. . . .

III. Psychological eudaimonism in contrast to rational eudaimonism, requires the *rejection* of . . . possibilities that common sense recognizes: common sense believes that it is possible for us *to benefit someone else* for the other *person's own sake, not for our own happiness.* (1994, 53)

Let us proceed to study these questions more closely: what does Socrates mean by 'happiness' in the first place? And exactly whose happiness is at stake? Finally, what is the relationship between Socrates' intellectualism, his insistence that knowledge of the good leads to virtue, and his endaimonism.

According to the account we have been following, the Socratic search for knowledge of the good is related to a thesis about the overall end of action, which is happiness, although that end is conceived vaguely at best; after all, what is happiness? For unless we can say something about what this will look like, we won't have any idea where all of this searching, defining, examining and refuting is taking us. The word 'happiness' that Socrates presents, as we have seen, as the self-evident end for all human action, fails to specify whether we are talking about subjective or objective conditions. Is happiness a pre-reflective concept that just equates with our ordinary understanding of happiness, one that accommodates the actual diversity of human desire, or is it, rather, prescriptive of the human good? It would seem that the question Aristotle raises in the *NE* also applies to these Socratic texts:

> Most people are pretty much agreed about the name [of the final good]; for both the many and the refined call it happiness, and suppose that living well and doing well are the same as being happy. But as to what happiness is, they disagree, and the many do not characterize it in the same way as the wise. (1095a17–26)[3]

We must also consider whose happiness is at stake when we read such texts as *Euthydemus* 278d4. From the fact that each of us desires to be happy, are we entitled to infer that each should; therefore, pursue his or her own happiness first and foremost? Or is this rather a fact to keep in mind about other people, that they desire to be happy, and therefore we ought to respect their claims, desires, needs and well-being as well as our own?

In the *Apology*, Socrates says deliberation should take into account only 'whether one is doing things that are just or unjust, or the acts of a good or a bad man' (33a1). Socrates lists a number of reasons for acting, including 'care of the soul', the 'examined life', 'virtue' and 'the actions of a just man' (32ab). Perhaps the most important stimulus for his entry into the philosophical life and his commitment to remain in this profession is what Socrates says at *Apology* 21b, the fact that he thought it his duty to 'come to the aid of the god' in determining the meaning of the oracle's answer to Chaeredemus' question: is there anyone wiser than Socrates? The one reason for acting that Socrates does not mention in the *Apology* is '*eudaimonia*, his own or others'.

Taking stock, we have seen multiple avenues for approaching the topic of Socratic ethics. It is intellectualist, at least to some extent, in relying on a search for definition and assuming that there is a strong correlation between having a virtue and knowing the good. Moreover, it is associated with eudaimonism, in the sense that there are several Socratic dialogues that take the end of all rational action to be happiness. Finally, it is virtue-centred insofar as, right from the beginning, Socrates claims that he does nothing 'other than going around to each [Athenian] like a father or elder brother, admonishing them to pursue nothing other than virtue' (*Ap*. 31b). So what we need now is an account of how all three terms – knowledge, virtue and happiness – can be shown to coincide in Socratic ethics.

What is the relationship between *eudaimonia*, well-being, and *arête*, virtue? The position that virtue is completely or partially constitutive of happiness is one kind of answer.[4] The position that virtue is instrumental to happiness is another kind of answer.[5]

THE CONCEPT OF THE 'BENIGN EGOIST': PROBLEMS WITH INSTRUMENTALISM

Let us proceed to examine first instrumentalism and its varieties as they appear in recent work on Socrates. As we saw with the quote from Irwin, when Socrates claims that everyone wishes to be happy, or that all desire is for the good, the standard interpretation takes these statements to imply that Socrates subscribes to the thesis of egoistic eudaimonism.[6] At its most extreme formulation, this kind of interpretation does not even make Socrates out to be a moral philosopher at all. Instead, if anything, Socrates was a psychologist who discovered that, at root, all human beings seek their *own* happiness, whether or not they are aware of it. For Socrates, according to this thesis, it is impossible for an individual to be motivated to do anything other than what is in his or her interest.

For students of ancient philosophy, a review of this topic is to be found in Kraut (1989). According to Kraut, 'pure egoism' is a doctrine that holds that all legitimate reasons for action will maximize the agent's own good. Therefore, the good of others will hold no independent weight, although, of course, there may be self-serving or self-interested reasons for treating others well, insofar as such treatment is conducive to one's own optimal good. Another form of egoism can be called 'benign egoism', the thesis that 'denies that the good of one person can conflict with another' (Kraut 1989, 81). The benign egoist 'insists that no one will be worse off if we maximize our own good and assign priority to self-interested reasons', just because in some ways the welfare of others will be a part of one's own interest or own happiness. Socrates is most often thought to be a benign egoist. For example, Reshotko (2006, 58) writes that 'Socrates thinks that harm and benefit are always and only harm or benefit to the self. . . . Socrates thinks that whenever an individual chooses to act, she chooses the particular, available, action that she thinks will bring her the most benefit.' Nevertheless, according to these interpreters,

Socrates believes that harming another never benefits an agent. This Socrates comes off as likeable in the extreme: he enlarges the scope of what counts as self-interest so that, apparently, it inevitably, invariably and necessarily includes the interests of others. Socrates is precisely a benign egoist. These interpreters frame Socratic egoism so that it encompasses the other-regarding virtues. In other words, Socratic eudaimonism is, in the last analysis, a virtue-centred ethics. Now we see in what sense virtue is said to be instrumental to happiness in the view that ascribes eudaimonism to Socrates; virtue – that is, knowledge of the good – is what allows people to achieve happiness. Moreover, since other-regarding virtues allow one to use wisdom to assist others in securing happiness, in this sense happiness is impossible without virtue (wisdom, or knowledge of the good).

Therefore the question arises, if Socratic egoism is framed in such an attractive way, such that it encompasses the other-regarding virtues and construes well-being so broadly that the interests of those around one are always taken into account, or at least should be, what objections could one mount against it? Surely one could not attack the thesis on the grounds that, for example, Socrates engages in other-directed activity, values his friends and is devoted to the well-being of his community. For all of these possibilities will be included in the benign egoism, construed in the broadest possible way, that is attributed to Socrates. There are two problems with this instrumentalist interpretation of Socratic virtue: there is no evidence that Socrates thinks that people act in order to benefit themselves primarily, and the conception of happiness at stake here is so thin as to be singularly unilluminating. Let us study the first problem, the problem of reason ascription. Why, we want to ask Socrates, do people act? Is it always to make themselves happy? Almost astonishingly, Vlastos writes:

> Here desire for happiness is strictly self-referential: it is the agent's desire for his own happiness and that of no one else. This is so deep seated an assumption that it is simply taken for granted: no argument is ever given for it in the Platonic corpus.[7]

Indeed, no argument is ever given for what amounts to an assumption that is not only counter-intuitive but also implausible as a reading of the Socratic dialogues: we commonly understand conceptions such as self-sacrifice, beneficence and duty as valid descriptions of actions, and Socrates also uses this kind of language to describe his own actions.

I would argue that Socrates is not an egoist precisely because he does not think that the reasons for actions can best be captured in terms of whether they are primarily self-beneficial. Sometimes Plato represents Socrates as acting because he wishes to promote the well-being of others, irrespective of whether this activity will benefit himself. Again, sometimes Plato represents Socrates as acting because of the demands of justice, for the sake of the truth or for the sake of the good. Nowhere does Plato represent Socrates as acting for his own sake primarily, exclusively or in a self-interested way.

Since, for Socrates, in knowing justice we become just and consequently act justly towards others, virtue involves doing good to others, quite apart from whether such action benefits oneself. As Socrates puts the matter at *Gorgias* 460b8–10:

> SOCRATES: Isn't a man who has learned what's just a just man too?
>
> GORGIAS: Yes, absolutely.
>
> SOCRATES: And a just man does just things, I take it.

In the *Apology*, Socrates describes his philosophical activity in the following way: 'the Olympian victor makes you think yourself happy; I make you be happy' (36e9). But if Socrates says that what he is doing is making others happy, then how can we construe his version of eudaimonism as egoistic? In fact, one of the least-studied aspects of Plato's Socrates is the concern that Socrates shows for the welfare of all the members of his community; the *Apology* even contains a number of statements that appear to be primarily other-regarding. For example, at 36, the Athenians require that Socrates suggest a counter-proposal to his capital sentence, whereupon Socrates insists that what he ought to have from the state is a reward, since he has spent his life 'conferring upon each citizen individually what [he] regard[s] as the greatest benefit'.

The second problem with instrumentalism is that it leaves the constituents, contents and nature of happiness unspecified. Let us recall the radical distinction that Socrates invokes in the *Euthydemus*: 'all other things [apart from wisdom] are neither good nor bad.' States of affairs in the world, Socrates is saying here, are in themselves neither-good-nor-bad; instead people should value, literally 'care for', their souls, since virtue is the source of all genuine good for human beings (*Ap.* 30b2). Socrates shows us that even death and poverty are in themselves neither-good-nor-bad (*Ap.* 31; 37).[8] In other words, wise use of things is to see them as neither-good-nor-bad. Death and poverty form ingredients of Socrates' overall good, even though they represent the extreme absence of any external goods.

Now, it is often said that Socrates recommends virtue on the grounds that virtues benefit the person who possesses them.[9] In the *Laches*, Socrates says that bravery is a virtue, and so must always be fine and beneficial (192c4–b5); in the *Charmides*, Socrates says that temperance is a good (160e9). But in neither of these texts does Socrates specify that virtue benefits the person who possesses it. In fact, he does not specify whom the virtue benefits at all. Rather, he suggests that one who has virtue is good: 'temperance must be a good if it makes those good in whom it is present, and makes bad those in whom it is not' (*Ch.* 161a6). With this conception of happiness in mind, then, a conception that is strongly linked to virtue, we can turn once more to texts like the *Gorgias*, where Socrates talks a great deal about happiness, or, at least, he tries to show what happiness is not.

'HAPPINESS' IN THE *GORGIAS*

Polus is a younger disciple of Gorgias who openly vaunts rhetoric as the art of persuasion with words. It enables its practitioners to get what they want. And so those who use the art of rhetoric have the most power, and thus are the happiest people. The elenchus with Polus begins at 467c. Socrates applies the prudential principle, that everyone wants good things, to an analysis of action: we do some things for the sake of other things, as means to achieve our ends, those things for the sake of which we act, that is, good things (468a–b). Thus, when people gain power and are able to put people to death, to exile them and to confiscate their property, they do so in order to secure good things (468b). But suppose that these actions result in consequences that are not beneficial to those who perform them. In this case, people who have great power can do as they wish, though not necessarily as they want (468c). Polus is not impressed by this answer: he asks Socrates whether those who put people to death and confiscate property are happy or not. Socrates replies that if they do so justly, then he feels sorry for them, but if they do so unjustly, then they are the most wretched of all people.

In calling attention to the distinction between doing what seems best to one and truly wanting something, Socrates is trying to show that no one who does what is wrong does so willingly, that is, wanting those results. More generally, then, the conclusion will coincide with what Socrates says elsewhere (*Prot.* 345e1–2): no human being errs willingly. Now we can begin to see what use this less egoistic, more virtue-oriented reading of the Socratic dialogues makes of eudaimonism, the thesis that everyone desires well-being. The idea is that committing injustice, harming others or doing wrong, is harmful not just for the putative victim, but much more so for the one who commits the wrong. The Socratic thesis, then, is that wrongdoing is bad for the person who does wrong; therefore, it is in our interests, paradoxically, not to pursue self-interest at the expense of others.

In our dialogue, Socrates goes on to show Polus that 'neither I nor you nor any man whatever would rather do than suffer wrong, for to do it is worse' (475e5). Here Socrates says that it is worse to do than to receive injustice, but he leaves it unclear as to whether committing injustice is worse for the agent, for his or her victim, or simply worse in some non-consequential, ethical sense that has to do with the idea of moral badness or wrongness. Now, the literature on this passage is vast, and many scholars have concluded that the agreement Socrates secures with Polus turns on an equivocation in the argument.[10] Polus admits that doing injustice is more shameful than being the recipient of injustice, but he wants to maintain that it can nevertheless actually be good to, for example, kill with impunity (469c). The argument exploits various shades of value that attend the Greek words for shameful (*aischron* – a word that also has the connotation of 'aesthetically displeasing') and for beautiful (*kalon* – a word that also has the sense of 'noble, respectable') and the more generic word for good (*agathon* – a word that veers towards moral value but can denote utility as well) that are used in the evaluation of just and unjust actions.

Despite the prolific discussion on how ambiguity figures into the dialectic, in the end Socrates' point seems clear enough; Socrates returns to the familiar topos of the intrinsic badness of injustice in the soul, on the analogy with poor health of the body: to commit injustice is to worsen the condition of the soul.[11] Socrates' strategy against Polus ultimately involves the eudaimonist weighing of the consequences of injustice. In this case, Polus is self-deceived when he thinks that people are securing their own good when they commit injustices.

Another such text is *Crito* 49b. Socrates makes clear that the principle that one ought never to commit injustice is unrelated to any consequences for the agent:

> whether we must endure still more grievous sufferings than these, or lighter ones, is not wrongdoing inevitably an evil and a disgrace to the wrongdoer? Do we believe this or not?

In our text, Socrates emphasizes that this agreement not to harm will be the starting point of deliberation. He is going to argue from this premise and determine which action (escaping or remaining in prison) might be consistent with this underlying assumption. Nevertheless, those who wish to emphasize the priority of eudaimonist considerations operating in the sphere of the Socratic injunction not to harm often cite *Crito* 51, 'and will life be worth having, if that higher part of man be depraved, which is improved by justice and deteriorated by injustice?' Here the argument is that a person who commits injustice harms his soul, so that his life, under the circumstances of committing injustice, is not worth living. Hence he, the agent of the justice or injustice, is better off refraining from injustice.

Thus we may summarize what we have uncovered of Socratic ethics as follows, beginning from the Socratic thesis that virtue is knowledge: one who knows the good does the good. While doing the good, one does the good for others as well as oneself and equally along with oneself. In contrast, one who does not know the good does not (cannot) do the good. While not doing the good, one harms both oneself and others. As Plato puts it in the *Republic*: 'it is the function not of the just person to harm either a friend or anyone else, but of his opposite, the unjust person' (335d11).

SOCRATES' SERVICE TO HIS FELLOW HUMAN BEINGS

Before concluding this chapter on Socratic ethics, it will be necessary to glance at a fatal flaw in all of this speculation concerning what, if anything, can be known about the ethical teachings of Socrates on the basis of Plato's Socratic dialogues. From the very beginning, Socrates denies that he has knowledge of wisdom, that he knows anything fine or good, and that he has knowledge of virtue. How, then, can Socrates avoid this very same harm, both for himself and for others, that, he warns, is the consequence of not having wisdom, of not knowing the good? Even if Socrates tries to avoid wrongdoing by not catering to his own desires for things that he recognizes are neither-good-nor-bad, and so avoids common mistakes like greed, ambition and violence through the realization that so-called goods like wealth, power and even life itself are no more good than bad, what benefit can others derive from his exhortation to virtue if the knowledge of the good, on which it depends, can never be found? Recall that we saw precisely this complaint in the pseudo-Platonic *Clitophon*: 'I came to the conclusion that while you're better than anyone at turning a man towards the pursuit of virtue, one of two things must be the case: either this is all you can do and nothing more, there are only two possibilities . . . either you don't know [sc. what justice is] or you don't wish to share it with me' (410e).

Clitophon is disappointed because Socrates seemed to promise more than he could deliver: Socrates pointed to the urgent need we all have for knowledge of virtue, but then seemed to suggest that this knowledge was out of reach. As a result, Clitophon has gone off to study with Thrasymachus. Maybe even worse than finding Socrates a huge disappointment is coming to hate Socrates because of the shortcomings he exposes in his interlocutors. Are all of these problems due to Socrates' endorsement of an intellectualist ethics? If so, the point is not lost on Socrates himself, who recalls his life of elenctic examination for the jury when he says: 'as a result of this investigation, men of Athens, I acquired much unpopularity, of a kind that is hard to deal with and is a heavy burden' (*Ap.* 23a). So far we have seen that Socrates inducts other members of his community into the examined life; the lack of any recognizable expertise in human affairs foists on all members of the community the same requirement, to grapple with how things seem to them, how they feel, what they want and what everyone else is doing, and instead try to see how things are. We have also seen that what get in the way of this responsibility are the opinions that everyone hands out. In the *Protagoras*, Socrates compares listening to the words of so-called teachers of wisdom with ingesting poison. Socrates is not handing out anything. There is nothing to fear from him, even though he does not have the knowledge of virtue he demands from himself and others. One may go away hungry from his feasts, and we saw this was true of Clitophon, but this is better than going to a typical intellectual repast and leaving stuffed with junk food.

FURTHER READING

Penner, T. and Rowe, C. 2005. *Plato's Lysis*. Cambridge: Cambridge University Press. Advocates understanding Socratic ethics as a strictly egoistic form of eudaimonism.

Weiss, R. 2005. *The Socratic Paradox and Its Enemies*. Chicago, IL: University of Chicago Press. Argues the contrary view, that Socrates is neither an egoist nor a eudaimonist.

CHAPTER SEVEN

THE SOCRATIC SCHOOLS

THE IMPORTANCE OF SOCRATES' PERSONAL CONDUCT AND BELIEFS TO THE HELLENISTIC SCHOOLS

We have devoted the previous two chapters to discussing philosophy as theory, as dependent on doctrine, and as a testing of the truth of propositions. In doing so, we have veered away from what virtually all of the ancients, with the exception of Aristotle, saw as the essence of Socratic philosophy, which was the philosophical or examined life, or perhaps even the art of living as opposed to the science of happiness that was the particular interpretation of Aristotle. Especially for the Hellenistic schools, philosophy as a whole, as Cicero puts it, comes down from the heavens and becomes a matter of helping human beings achieve a kind of life worth living, the good life. These schools all specified an end or goal for life (*telos* in Greek) and made that goal the basis of a philosophical practice. Dialectic, doctrine, propositions – these have their place in the philosophical life, which is always a life of reason, yet they do not occupy the whole of it; indeed, it was possible to construct at least the basis for practising the philosophical life even in the absence of absolute knowledge. In this respect, at least, Hellenistic philosophy relied more on the figure of Socrates than on the theories of Platonism.

The Stoics, along with the Cynics and Sceptics, are among the Hellenistic schools of philosophy that deliberately adopted Socrates as their common ancestor and exemplar; the Stoics and Sceptics, especially, read and assimilated the Socratic dialogues of Plato, finding templates for their own extremely divergent realizations of happy lives

SOCRATES: A GUIDE FOR THE PERPLEXED

or, we might better say, lives lived with integrity. Just as the Stoics valorized Socrates' indifference to death and poverty, so the Sceptics valorized Socrates' disavowal of knowledge in their construction, or rather reconstitution, of a Socratic life that could be the object of imitation for everyone. But before we get to these later appropriations of Socratic philosophy, we must return once more to events within Socrates' own lifetime to trace the origins of the 'Socratic schools', philosophers who deliberately attempted to take on the mantle of Socrates.

What I show in this chapter is how one distinctive feature of Socratic philosophy, namely Socrates' targeting of *doxa*, opinion, became the theoretical foundation of the Hellenistic schools, even as his outward poverty and inner fortitude gave rise to Hellenistic ethics. Recall that Socrates spent his life pursuing those with a reputation for virtue and those with authority in the community. The Greek word for 'reputation' is *doxa*, which is the same Greek word that is used for 'belief', 'opinion' and 'point of view'. As we see in greater detail below, each of the Socratic schools assailed in its own way the ordinary person's reliance on *doxa*, on one's own opinions, preferences and feelings, in addition to conventional realizations of one's role and place in the community. Socrates' assault on *doxa*, in the form of criticizing his interlocutor's beliefs, undermining his moral authority, calling his credentials into question – all of this took place, as we saw, in a highly visible, public forum, in front of the city's youth, in front of colleagues, in the gymnasia where people congregated. The result of this public humiliation (recall that the original meaning of the word elenchus is to shame, humiliate) could well have been a significant loss of face. Now, one school in particular are associated with questioning ordinary values of propriety, of convention, of honour itself, and these were the Cynics, or Dogs. It is with their story that we begin.

THE CYNICS

We have already become familiar in chapter three with the succession story told in Diogenes Laertius' *Lives of the Eminent Philosophers*, which posits an unbroken chain of teaching from Socrates through Antisthenes, Diogenes, Crates and Zeno, thus making Socrates the 'father of the dogs' (Cynics) through Antisthenes, and the great-great grandfather of the Stoics, through Crates, the first teacher of Zeno, who founded the Stoa.[1] In his *Life of Antisthenes* (6.13) Diogenes Laertius tries to document Antisthenes' credentials for being the first Cynic:

> [Antisthenes] used to hold discussions in the gymnasium at Cynosarges not far from the gates, whence some [conclude] that the Cynic school derived its name from that district. And he was the first, Diocles tells us, to double his cloak and be content with that one garment and to take up a staff and a wallet.

Here Antisthenes is portrayed as inventing the signature costume of the Cynics, necessitated by their voluntary poverty and homelessness. What is important for us is not the literal truth of the master–disciple tradition, which is rightly disputed, but instead the way that Antisthenes, perhaps the oldest member of the Socratic circle and one of the earliest Socratics to publish Socratic literature, is said to have inaugurated the Cynics endorsement of poverty, already anticipated by Socrates, as well as their trademark shamelessness. Although Antisthenes is mentioned only once by name in Plato's works, in the deathbed scene of the *Phaedo*, Antisthenes is given a major speaking part in Xenophon's Socratic works as a fond, and even fanatical, follower of Socrates. In Xenophon's *Symposium* IV.34–44 (*SSR* VA 82), Antisthenes delivers a 'sermon' that has a Cynic feel on the virtues of poverty: he discovers the natural limit for appetite and so avoids what he calls 'the distressing disease' of those who are in the constant grip of desire for 'more', where 'more' is experienced as, by definition, without limit. Antisthenes has wealth in his soul, the inner storehouse; as for those who are addicted to wealth and power, these people show, in their condition of constant need, inner poverty. In his speech, Antisthenes makes a point of thanking Socrates: 'Socrates here, from whom I obtained it [my inner wealth, or poverty] didn't supply me by quantity or weight, but handed over to me as much as I could carry away.' There are echoes here of Plato's *Apology* in this praise of poverty – as for example, 'I live in great poverty because of my service to the god' (23c1).

Antisthenes is said to have taught that 'evil is constituted by everything that is foreign' (DL vi.12). And in Epictetus we read:

> Since the time that Antisthenes set me free, I have no longer been a slave . . . he taught me [the distinction between] what is mine and

what is not mine. Property is 'not mine'. Relatives, servants, friends, reputation, accustomed haunts, pastimes, [he taught] are foreign.[2]

The renunciation of possessions extends past external wealth: it is also a kind of inner freedom and autonomy, a self-reliance that sees past social convention, with its endless requirement that people amass 'more' wealth, knowledge, power, etc.

Traditionally, the first philosopher to play the part of the dog was Diogenes of Sinope, of course. Plato is said to have called Diogenes 'a Socrates gone mad', no doubt for his guerrilla style of doing philosophy – a mixture of interactive satire and street theatre. Diogenes surpassed Antisthenes in his pursuit of what the Greeks called *autarkeia*, self-sufficiency, as the anecdotal tradition reflects: Diogenes elevated homelessness to a philosophical art by adopting a storage jar belonging to the temple of Cybele as his shelter (vi.23); he threw away his wooden bowl after seeing a boy drinking from his hands (vi.37); when rebuked for masturbating in the market-place he answered: 'If only it was as easy to soothe my hunger with a stroke of the hand' (vi.41). Antisthenes in Xenophon's *Symposium* boasts that he sleeps with any woman who happens to be at hand; Diogenes goes one better by not requiring a partner. Antisthenes is content to live in a modest house; Diogenes lives in a wine barrel.

This living in the open is related to other Cynic values, to Cynic 'shamelessness' (*anaideia*), a rejection of the routine acceptance of convention as a false consciousness that substitutes for genuine virtue. Again, we see the Socratic undertones of these Cynic practices, with Antisthenes playing perhaps a kind of intermediary role. For example, Socrates goes up to Nicias, leader of the Athenian military expedition against Southern Italy, and finds that he doesn't know what courage is. When asked in which part of Greece he had met with 'real men', Diogenes is said to have responded: 'Men nowhere but I saw boys in Sparta' (DL VI. 27). The quest for the real meaning of our conventional language seems related to the Socratic search for the definition of virtue. It is as if Socrates is searching among generals, trying to find one who can embody the martial virtue of courage, just as, among Spartan warriors, Diogenes looks for real men: the Greek word for 'courage', *andreia*, manly virtue, is etymologically connected to the root, *andreis*, 'men'.

In his writings, Antisthenes already more than hints at something of Cynic ethics: evidently, one of his sayings was 'the beginning of education is the examination of names'. This saying should remind us of Socrates' elenchus as well as Diogenes' search for men. Clearly, Antisthenes' doubted the possibility of definition, as Aristotle reports: 'you cannot define what a thing is "for a definition is a long logos" though you can teach what it is like, (*Meta.* 1943b23–32).' Virtue is more than just theory; we must find the substance behind the jargon. Diogenes is said to have walked into a classroom in which Plato was lecturing, holding up a plucked chicken and crying: 'behold Plato's man' (featherless biped: vi.40). Likewise, Antisthenes is said to have remarked: 'you don't need theory to be virtuous.' The inner strength of the wise person, his fortitude and self-reliance, all of this is seen in the legends surrounding Socrates' feats of strength, walking through the snows of winter unshodden, and in the Cynic and Antisthenean adoption of Hercules as the example of a virtuous person, because of his toil.

THE HELLENISTIC AND ROMAN STOA

If imitating the life of Socrates, his constant toil on behalf of wisdom, his indifference to wealth and even death itself, inspired what Cynics called their *askesis*, their 'training' in wisdom, then perhaps it was only a matter of time until this indifference itself became a goal of training, even, construed properly, wisdom itself. Such at any rate is how the Stoics understood the inner life of the sage, negatively expressed, as freedom from passions: literally, *apatheia*. Moreover, this indifference corresponded to a Stoic system of valuation that was directly informed by the Stoics' reading of Plato's Socratic dialogues. We have already introduced *Euthydemus* 281d2–e5 and have seen how crucial it is for understanding Socratic ethics: everything other than wisdom is neither-good-nor-bad. Wisdom alone is good. Moreover, it is good for the very reason that virtue is knowledge or wisdom, and virtue is the only basis for a happy life:

> In sum, I said, it looks like this, Cleinias: as for all the things which at first we said are good, our argument concerning them is not this – that they are by nature good in themselves. Rather this appears to be how things stand; that if ignorance leads them, they are greater bads than their opposites, to the extent that they are more able to serve what leads, it being bad, while if intelligence and wisdom lead, they are greater goods, but in themselves neither of them is worth anything. What then is the consequence of what

has been said? Is it anything other than that of all the other things, none is either good or bad, but as to these two things, wisdom is good, ignorance bad? – He agreed.

This passage (also quoted on p. 82) is related to a more formal Stoic scheme according to which all things are evaluated on the basis of how they contribute to the goal of life, which is just virtue, wisdom or a life lived according to wisdom, which the Stoics variously called 'living according to nature' or 'living harmoniously'. The Stoics openly teach what Socrates implies, that, in the words of Diogenes Laertius:

> some existing things are good, others are bad, and others are neither of these. The virtues – prudence, justice, courage, moderation and the rest – are good. The opposites of these – foolishness, injustice, and the rest – are bad. Everything which neither does benefit nor harm is neither of these; for instance, life, health, pleasure beauty, strength, wealth, reputation, noble birth and their opposites, death, disease, pain, ugliness, weakness, poverty, low repute, ignoble birth and the like. (vii.101–2)

We saw that Socrates says in the *Apology* that 'a good man' cannot be harmed. The Roman Stoic Epictetus, who lived some six hundred years after Socrates, still took Socrates to be the guide of life.

Epictetus' *Handbook* ends with a kind of paraphrase of this idea: Meletus and Anytus may kill me, but they cannot harm me.[3] The idea is that the good is what benefits and what only benefits. But since, as is implied in the *Euthydemus* passage, everything – wealth, health, life itself – may be used for harm or for benefit, virtue alone may be considered truly good.[4]

The Stoics introduce a distinction, one that need not detain us for long here, according to which, owing to a creature's natural desire to preserve itself, some, things are amenable for preservation (e.g. organic vegetables; health more generally), while others things are not (e.g. Cheese Whiz; disease more generally). The former are 'preferred' indifferents; the latter are 'dispreferred'. Another way that the Stoics talk about them is to say that some things have 'selective' value, meaning that we tend to choose them, all things being equal, while other things do not have selective value, meaning that we tend to avoid them, all things being equal. Yet in neither case do any indifferents have absolute value or intrinsic merit.

The full classificatory scheme entailed by Stoic ethics is as follows:

Stoic theory of value

GOOD	Virtue
BAD	Vice
INDIFFERENTS	All that is not virtue or vice
Preferred INDIFFERENTS	Things in accord with nature
Not preferred INDIFFERENTS	Things not in accord with nature

Now, with these distinctions in place, it is crucial to discuss the attitude that one should have towards ordinary things in the world, the things that occupy most human beings most of the time: health, wealth, reputation and so forth. We saw that Antisthenes defined these as foreign and that the Cynics positively eschewed them as not complementary to their poverty, as providing distractions from the leisure they gained by not attending to them. What of the Stoics? While it may be that in labelling these so-called goods 'preferred' the Stoics distance themselves from the perfect 'indifference' of Socrates and the Cynics, what is crucial for the Stoics is the attitude of the mind in approaching these objects, which ought never to be objects of desire or aversion for the sage. Grasping at a thing as constituting a good and therefore taking pleasure in it (say, winning the lottery), recoiling from a thing as constituting an evil and thereby being pained it (say, losing one's job), eagerly anticipating a thing and desiring it as a future good (having a child) or dreading something as a future evil (becoming old and frail) – all of these are outright mistakes of judgement. Indeed, all emotions are the result of wrong opinions, lack of knowledge about what, as Socrates puts it in the *Laches*, 'is to be feared or hoped for'. There is only one thing good, and that is virtue; one thing bad, and that is vice.

For the early Stoa (the Stoa of Zeno and Chrysippus) the emotions originated as cognitive dispositions to evaluate states of affairs in terms of the advantage or disadvantage that they possessed. Desire equated with the belief that a certain situation was inherently good; fear, in turn, equated with the belief that a certain situation was inherently bad. All emotions – for example, greed, anger, lust, cowardice – flow from this one central channel, namely the belief that states of affairs can be, in themselves, either good or bad.[5] Not so for the Stoics. In fact there was only one good, moral virtue, and one bad, moral vice. These terms, then ('good' and 'bad'), refer in the strict sense only to states of affairs in the human soul. Every other state of affairs, that is conditions or objects of infinite variety, falls technically under the heading of 'indifferent', meaning that no absolute value can be ascribed to it.[6]

The sage alone is able to treat indifferent things as truly indifferent; ordinary people experience emotions as a result of their ability or inability to acquire items in the category of indifferents.[7] Therefore, the Stoic sage is able to see things from the point of view of Zeus. All things form part of a seamless universal nexus of events, the *hiemarmene,* or fate, that is identical with the body and will of Zeus, the ultimate rational principle. Although every human mind is a spark, or *apospasma,* of this rational principle, only the sage is able to live a life in accord with this fact. The sage alone recognizes that since all things are willed by Zeus, this universe is the best possible world. Everything that happens within this world is necessarily a part of the total perfection. Stoic philosophy is designed, at the highest end of the philosophical spectrum, to help the practitioner acquire the mind of the sage who constantly attends to the perfection.[8] Epictetus' favourite saying was:

Lead me, Zeus, and you, Fate, wherever you have ordained for me. For I shall follow unflinching. But if I become bad and unwilling, I shall follow none the less. (*Enchiridion* 53, from Cleanthes' Hymn to Zeus)

Sagacity is the *summum bonum* of the Stoic school. The sage represents the human quest for perfection, expressed in the Platonic curriculum as the very culminating stage of one's studies, when one attains 'likeness to god': the very concept of the sage looks backwards in time to the charismatic influence of Socrates.

As Long points out, Epictetus' own experience of slavery surfaced in his lifelong habit of taunting his freeborn students with the jibe 'slave'. His style with the interlocutors who appear in the *Discourses* is rough, haranguing and in the manner of the Cynic diatribe:

I have to die! Do I also have to die groaning? *I have to be fettered.* While moaning too? *I have to go into exile.* Does anyone prevent me from going with a smile, cheerful and serene? *Tell your secrets.* I refuse, because that is up to me. *Then I will fetter you.* What do you mean, fellow? Fetter me? You can fetter my leg but not even Zeus can overcome my volition. (1.121–3)

Epictetus, like his spiritual ancestor Socrates, taught groups of wealthy youths in public, writing nothing, but directly ministering to the spiritual needs of his students. His was a philosophy of self-transformation consistent with the Socratic exhortation to virtue. Perhaps the greatest affinity with Socrates, however, lay in Epictetus' emphasis on the god within.

In Greek, the word that Epictetus uses as the focal point for his philosophical instruction is *prohairesis*.[9] We might literally translate this word as 'choice', which in turn implies the freedom to choose. But for Epictetus, *prohairesis* refers to the authentic self, the character that one has come to form, and the possibility realizing one's identity as an *apospasma* (spark) of Zeus:

> My friend, you have a *prohairesis* that is by nature unimpeded and unconstrained. This is inscribed here in the entrails. I will prove it to you, first in the sphere of assent. Can anyone prevent you from assenting to a truth? No one can. Can anyone compel you to accept a falsehood? No one can. (*M*1.17.21–4)

This faculty of assent is fundamental to the whole structure of Stoic psychology and epistemology. In assent (Greek *katathesis*) lies the essence of our rationality and the essence of our freedom.[10] It is the faculty of assent that distinguishes humans from other animals and hence brings us into the sphere of the divine. One way of understanding this faculty is to consider that, for the Stoics, there are actually two parts to any given thought. The first aspect is the presentation (Greek *phantasia*), which is something like a thusness or so-ness. All thoughts flow through the mind as presenting certain qualities. The other part is the affirmation, the assent to the presentation as true. The affirmation is like an inner voice that stamps a kind of inner commitment on the presentation. This inner voice says: 'It *is* like this! This *is* how things truly are.' This ability to say 'yes' or to withhold our inner commitment is our *prohairesis*. For Epictetus this faculty, and only this faculty, lies in our power: no one can compel our inner commitment to the truth of an appearance. Epictetus identifies this inherent capacity to recognize the truth, the mind's inner light, as the inner deity:

Whenever you are in company, whenever you take exercise, whenever you converse, don't you know that you are nursing God,
exercising God? You are carrying God around, you poor things,
and you don't know it. (2.8.12–13)[11]

This rationality that Epictetus valorizes as a Socratic practice can now
be seen in terms of the Socratic interrogation of *doxa* that, we saw, was
the basis of the elenchus, and also as related to the Cynic repudiation
of *doxa* in the sense of reputation – external impression, the appearance of virtue in the guise of convention. In the Stoa, dialoguing with
one's *doxa*, with the appearance of things (actually the Stoics discussed
the practice of scrutinizing one's *phantasiai*, but the two words function in much the same manner), entails not merely being supremely
suspicious of *doxa*, but eschewing it altogether: the sage does not
opine. It is this targeting of *doxa* as the weakest link, so to speak, in the
chain of wisdom for the sake of which the sage lives his life, which
resonates so strongly in the legacy of the Socratic persona.

For the Stoics, assent may be given or withheld, not only with
respect to propositions that harbour some truth-value about the
external world, but also with respect to any affective state that arises,
including desires and emotions. Dialoguing with a presentation or
mental state (the *phantasia* in Stoic parlance), ascertaining its origin,
gaining distance from the immediacy of its onset, all of this is a part
of Stoic psychological *askesis*, or practice. The goal of the Stoic
philosopher is to keep aloof from assenting to any presentation, any
mental state, whose truth-value could not survive under scrutiny. The
Stoic must also avoid assenting to presentations that might give rise
to emotional responses.

This aspect of Stoic psychology, its insistence on what we might
call psychic monism, posits that the emotions are due to value judge-
ments. Two kinds of these must be present for the person, according
to the Stoics, to undergo a full-scale emotional response: first, the
judgement that good or bad, benefit or harm, is present or immi-
nent, and, second, a kind of second-order judgement that decides
that it is appropriate to entertain the emotional response.[12] Socrates
too appears to offer a theory of psychic monism, or at least a way of
understanding pleasure, pain, fear and desire, which involves states
of knowledge and ignorance rather than affective states due to
separate motivational factors. In other words, Socrates apparently
rules out psychic conflict, one of the reasons that he can say that

virtue is knowledge. That is, if 'we' are somehow fundamentally knowers, not feelers or emotional reagents, then, according to Socrates, knowledge of what is truly good, rather than the resolution of any psychological conflict, will help us do what is good. Sometimes this understanding of the way that Socratic psychology works (and here the Stoics are very close) is called the 'denial of *akrasia*' or 'weakness of will'. Socrates says that what people call 'being overcome by pleasure' is a kind of mis-speaking: if pleasure is the good, then how, in choosing a lesser good (and so a lesser pleasure), will people actually be 'overcome' by pleasure? Rather, Socrates says, it is a matter of measuring accurately by means of whatever our criterion of good is; the rational capacity to measure, together with the art of measuring, will, Socrates says, 'prove to be our salvation in life' (*Prot.* 356e5).

Insofar as Hellenistic philosophers embrace the philosophy of Socrates, they appropriate both Socratic method, the elenchus, conceived as a testing or refutation of *doxa*, of opinion, and Socratic ethics, conceived as invulnerability, self-mastery, brought about precisely by the ability to see through, so to speak, one's own *doxai*, one's views, opinions, thoughts. We can now see how Socratic inquiry might inform Hellenistic philosophy, despite Socrates' disavowal of knowledge. Indeed, one well-known philosopher, Arcesilaus, who headed what was called the New Academy (c.273–c.242 BCE), actually claimed the Socratic disavowal of knowledge as the basis, not only of his philosophy, but of the good life. That he did so as a distortion and misreading of Plato's Socratic dialogues is very likely, as we shall see.

SCEPTICS AND THE NEW ACADEMY OF PLATO

The most important book for the history of Plato's Academy in the Hellenistic period is Cicero's dialogue the *Academica*.[13] Cicero counted himself a pupil of Philo of Larissa, *scholarch* or head of the Sceptical Academy in Cicero's student days, and in the *Academica* Cicero tries to present Philo's own version of how the Academy 'turned sceptical', that is emphasized the impossibility of knowledge rather than its actual pursuit. The story that Cicero tells, speaking for Philo of Larissa at *Academica* I. 44, mentions the Academic rivalry with the Stoic epistemology of Zeno and ends with a digression on Socrates:

> That's why Arcesilaus used to deny that anything could be known, not even the residual claim Socrates had allowed himself, i.e. the knowledge that he didn't know anything.

Scholars have pointed out how badly astray Cicero goes here in making Arcesilaus attribute to Socrates 'the knowledge that he didn't know anything', first because Socrates never says anything like this in the Socratic dialogues (he says that he has no *wisdom*, that he knows nothing *fine*, and that he is *conscious* of knowing nothing) and second because this affirmation of impossibility of knowledge goes against the Sceptical position, which is rather not to assent to anything as indubitably true without actual knowledge. In another passage of the *Academica*, we get a rather more accurate reflection of Socrates' position in the Socratic dialogues of Plato, when, making Varro the speaker, Cicero writes: 'Socrates was the first (this is a point accepted by all) to summon philosophy away from the obscure subjects nature has veiled. . . . His manner of argument is the same in practically all the conversations his students wrote up so eloquently and variously: he makes no affirmation of his own, but refutes other people and says that he knows nothing except just that.' (I.15–16 with omissions, Brittain trans. 92–3)

Here we see Arcesilaus' Sceptical interpretation of the relationship between Socratic method and Socratic wisdom: as a result of questioning those who think they know, Socrates comes to the conclusion that they do not know what they think they know. Socrates therefore practises a form of *ad hominem* argument that does not implicate him in any philosophical positions or force him to hold any beliefs.[14] Instead, Socrates simply shows that the interlocutor is unable to defend the position that he holds. And Cicero tells us that Arcesilaus 'revived [the method of] Socrates and made it a practice that those who wished to be his pupils should not inquire from him but should themselves say what they thought; when they had done so, he would argue against them' (*On Ends* 2.2, Cooper trans.; quoted by Cooper 2004, 91).

Although the Stoics certainly affirmed the truth of certain theses that they traced back to Socrates, for example that virtue is knowledge, that only virtue is good,[15] they shared with the Sceptics of the New Academy a disdain for opinion. What Arcesilaus seems to have done is apply Socratic dialectical method as he discovered it in the Socratic dialogues of Plato, finding a technique to refute the interlocutor's proposition without thereby committing himself to the truth of the counter-proposition. The Stoics, for their part, held that the sage would never opine, and therefore that the knowledge of the sage would keep him or her free from error. In theory, then, the Stoics affirm the possibility of knowledge. Yet the Stoic practitioner could ill afford to claim knowledge; the sage is as rare as the phoenix, and, apart from Socrates himself, it is unclear that any sages have actually appeared in history. Hence, like the Sceptic, the Stoic will never assent to any impression as absolutely true, but will approach all *phantasiai*, that is all *doxai*, mental states we could say, with caution.

Now, *aporia*, the realization that one does not know what one thought one knew, appears in the Socratic dialogues as a consequence of the joint search for truth with the interlocutor; it is not the stated goal of the elenchus, and Socrates reports the results of the failure to define terms in that search as a negative outcome, one that is a necessary part of progress towards the truth. Occasionally, it does seem that Socrates is willing to force his opponent into *aporia*, even when that person actually asserts a thesis that Socrates, on other occasions, appears to argue for. An example is the end of the *Laches*, where Nicias is shown that his definition of courage as 'knowledge of things fearful and hopeful' (194e11–195a1) entails 'knowledge of good and evil', and that this knowledge is the whole of virtue, not, as Nicias maintained courage was, a part of virtue (198a1). Yet in the *Protagoras*, Socrates apparently argues vehemently, if not altogether convincingly, for the truth of the paradoxical position, that all virtues are one. At the end of the dialogue, Socrates pretends that the argument he has just had with Protagoras addresses him reproachfully saying: 'Socrates, you earlier said that virtue cannot be taught but now you are arguing the very opposite and are attempting to show that everything is knowledge – justice, temperance, courage . . .' (361b1–3). Another example of Socrates refuting a definition or proposition that he seems elsewhere strongly to believe, endorse and even promulgate is the dialectical treatment of Critias' thesis at *Charmides* 164d4 and following, where Critias says that 'temperance is to know oneself'. By the end of the dialogue, Socrates has Critias concluding that temperance, if it is a knowledge of what one knows, or a science of science, 'won't be any benefit at all' (175a8). Why does Socrates, who elsewhere says that he is so busy trying to know himself, according to the Delphic precept, that he has no time for any other inquiry (*Phdr.* 230a1), deliberately sabotage

Critias' definition by construing this all important self-knowledge in a way that, apparently, renders it utterly useless?

These examples might lead a reader of Plato's Socratic dialogues to assume that *aporia* just is the goal of the elenchus – that Socrates' admission of ignorance, his own *aporia*, is the one thing that is transmissible to his interlocutors, even if virtue is not. In this sense, then, just as the Sceptics claimed to find 'tranquility' following suspension of belief (*epoche*), perhaps Socratic *aporia* might be affirmed as perspicuous in its own right, at least by a Sceptical reader of the Socratic dialogues such as Arcesilaus.

The contemporary reader cannot fail to be impressed by the Hellenistic fixation with Socrates. Even Socratic failures are counted as boons, as Socrates' signature ignorance is promoted as a goal in the case of the Sceptics. Even though, as we have seen, the Stoics could account for the destructive side of the Socratic method, in regarding as precipitate the assent to false impressions, and particularly the wrong kind of evaluative opinions that create emotional disturbance, leading the student astray from pursuit of virtue, the Stoics affirmed the Socratic thesis that virtue is knowledge and, indeed, modelled their entire psychology on this paradox. For them, the human mind itself was rational through and through; feelings, desires, emotions – all of these were variations on the rational state and could be moderated by the voice of reason. It is for this reason that Epictetus commended Socrates as the guide to life, telling his students: 'the person who can show each individual the conflict responsible for his error, and clearly make him see how he is not doing what he wants to do and is doing what he does not want to do – that is, the person who combines expertise in argument, exhortation and refutation' (3.12.15). For Epictetus, Socrates has these very qualities: just as Socrates used to say we should not live an unexamined life, so we should not accept an unexamined impression, but should say: wait, let me see who you are.[16]

ANTI-SOCRATIC PHILOSOPHY IN THE 'GARDEN' OF EPICURUS

One group of Hellenistic philosophers whom we have not yet talked about are the Epicureans. For them, it was not a question of Socratic wisdom or of Socratic ignorance, but of Socratic irony, that precisely disqualified Socrates from the practice of philosophy.[17] Not much is known about Epicurus' own views of Socrates; a quotation from Timocrates, an enemy of Epicurus, and found in Diogenes Laertius (X.7–8) attributes a sarcastic remark about Plato to Epicurus: 'Plato's school he called the "toadies of Dionysius", their master himself the "golden" Plato' (10.7–8). And Plutarch works hard to refute Epicurean criticisms of Platonic metaphysics, as we discover in his *Against Colotes*. What irked the Epicureans was precisely the Socratic profession of ignorance, insofar as Socrates did not attempt to persuade his 'students', if such they were, of the truth of any of his doctrines, if indeed he had any. Epicureans, on the other hand, relied on recruitment techniques that might be compared to propaganda, as for example the sculpting of statues of Epicurus that would have exuded a charismatic force.[18] When we first open Lucretius' poem *De rerum natura*, the proem stands out as something as far removed from Socrates or even Plato's reports of Socrates as one could imagine. For Lucretius, there is no doubt that Epicurus has discovered the Truth with a capital T, the answer to what ails human beings, and the sole remedy for ignorance. The only task left is to persuade the student of the truth of Epicurus' teaching (*DRN* I.50). According to Diogenes (DL 10.121) Epicurus purportedly says the very antithesis of what we have seen in the Stoic reception of Socrates when he states that 'the wise man will dogmatize, not suspend judgment' (Riley 1980, 58).

For explicit criticisms of Socrates himself, we must turn to the fragmentary treatises of Philodemus, an Epicurean poet, litterateur and philosopher, many of whose works survived the eruption of Vesuvius in the library at Piso's Villa of the Papyri in Herculaneum. One of the treatises recovered from the charred bits of papyri painstakingly reconstructed by papyrologists is a work titled *On Vices*. Philodemus lists various kinds of arrogance with an eye to helping the student remove them (he also uses material from a renegade Stoic, Aristo of Chios, a fact that complicates the work). Socrates is the *Eiron*, the dissimulator, par excellence: he does not say what he thinks; he criticizes and belittles himself and others; he attributes his own views to others. Elsewhere, for example in his treatise 'On Frank Speech', Philodemus gives an account of how the genuine philosopher should relate to those who undertake philosophy with him: he should recognize that he is their only saviour; he should criticize them openly and generally act as a physician who will heal his patients of the disease of falsehood. But if Socrates claims that he has no wisdom, that he can help no one, and, further, if his outrage over, even condemnation of, certain acts or views as entirely erroneous is only put forward in the guise of irony, then Socrates has no business claiming the mantle of philosopher.[19]

This survey of Hellenistic responses to Socrates has involved canvassing the different ways that each of the schools, Cynic, Stoic, Sceptic and Epicurean, responded to Socrates. In their interpretation of Socratic philosophy, the Stoics combined an appreciation of the Socratic critical elenchus with a more doctrinal understanding of Socratic ethics. From our perspective, we realize that in the divergent interpretations of the Stoa and the Academy, what is negotiated over and over again is the question of Socratic ignorance. How seriously are we to take it? And what limits does it place on Socrates' worth as a philosopher?

FURTHER READING

Annas, J. 2006. 'Plato the skeptic', in Ahbel-Rappe, S. and Kamtekar, R. eds. *A Companion to Socrates*. London: Blackwell.
Bett, R. 2006. 'Socrates and skepticism', in Ahbel-Rappe, S. and Kamtekar, R. eds. *A Companion to Socrates*. London: Blackwell.
Long, A. A. 1996. 'The Socratic tradition', in Branham, R. B. and Goulet-Cazé, M.-O., eds. *The Cynics: The Cynic Movement in Antiquity and Its Legacy.* Berkeley; Los Angeles, CA: University of California Press. 28–46. A ground-breaking essay on Socrates and Hellenistic philosophy. This rest of this volume is also an important resource on the Cynics in general.
—. 2002. *Epictetus.* Oxford: Oxford University Press. This treats of Socrates and Epictetus especially.
—. 2006. *From Epicurus to Epictetus.* Oxford: Oxford University Press.

CHAPTER EIGHT

SOCRATES IN THE MODERN WORLD

SOCRATIC PERSONAE

The competition between the Academy and the Stoa to claim Socrates as their own is an indication of just how difficult it was, even for those much closer than we are to the fourth century BCE, to construe the import of Socratic 'teaching' in light of Socrates' denial that he was ever a teacher (*Ap.* 19e1). Even the Stoics, who certainly had positive ethical teachings, and whose doctrinal formulations were shaped largely in terms of a debate with their Academic rivals, nevertheless emphasized the Socratic critique of *doxa*. In contrast, modern interpreters for the most part think of Socrates as promulgating a systematic ethics based on eudaimonism as a psychological thesis, and promoted through the deployment of elenctic principles. Today one finds in textbooks and monographs on Socrates such statements as 'Socrates taught the unity of the virtues', 'Socrates denied the possibility of *akrasia*', 'for Socrates, the only good is the agent's good' and similar dogmatic formulations. How different the modern approach is to the ancient spirit of interpretation should by now be clear. In this chapter, we study the trajectory that Socrates takes through the modern world, beginning with Hegel's introduction of Socrates as the inventor of ethical philosophy. We shall have occasion, below, to see what this invention entails, but for now it is necessary to undertake a digression to see the forces that shaped the modern interpretation of Socrates, beginning from the work of Plato himself. What I shall try to show in this chapter is how two competing tendencies, both stemming from Plato's treatment of the figure of Socrates, give rise to our modern understanding of Socrates. On the one hand, Socrates is an utterly unique individual, like no one else in fifth-century-BCE Athens, appearing on the streets and in the market-place, claiming to have an assignment from a god, able to heed the advice of a seemingly personal *daimonion*, given to bouts of trance, not clearly affiliated with any philosophical movement, but distancing himself from the trends current in his day. On the other hand, Socrates does exemplify, both in his life and in his philosophy, certain universal aspirations, if not exactly truths: the desire for happiness and well-being, the importance of virtue in the cultivation of a good life, the service of truth above what one happens to believe or what one's community tends to value.

No doubt part of the difficulty in reconciling the doctrinal Socrates with the aporetic Socrates lies in the Socratic traditions: Plato's Socrates versus Xenophon's Socrates, the Sceptics versus the Stoics, the Hellenistic Socrates versus the Aristotelian one, and so on. The divisions proliferate. And yet we have seen that Socrates is unique among philosophers because his life and death have mattered so much to us, in a way that is true, perhaps, only of characters in fiction and not generally of philosophers. Socrates the character is always in competition with Socrates the philosopher, for the reason that it is difficult to distinguish between Socratic philosophy and Socratic biography. All of those who reported on his philosophy were his biographers, and what they found so remarkable about him was his life. Socrates' silence perhaps forced his biographers into this position, and in this way Socrates was assured that we would never find his words orphaned from their author, yet, in an irony, in imitating the life of Socrates, philosophers find themselves constantly inventing Socrates' own inventions.

Whether we approach Socrates with a desire to theorize his irony, so that he may at last be transparent to us (the greatest reproach of the Epicureans was his lack of transparency), or whether we proclaim that Socrates' life is already transparent – resisting theory but functioning as the unique exemplar of invulnerability, or *epoche*, or simple decency – what we find is the difficulty that reproduces the ambiguity of our first sources, presenting Socrates in terms of the history of philosophy and presenting Socrates as a unique, inimitable individual who defies explanation. Seneca's Socrates is an example of the uniqueness tradition (*Epistle* I 6.6):

If you desire a model, take Socrates. That much-suffering old man was buffeted by every difficulty but still unconquered both by poverty (which his domestic burdens made more serious) and by labors (he also endured military service). He was harassed by these troubles at home, whether his wife, with her untamed character and impudent language, or his unlearned children, who were more like their mother than their father.

It is this feature of Socrates, that he lived a life somehow paradigmatic and yet at the same time inscrutable, that his wisdom was at once universal and yet intensely personal, that we find reflected in the modern receptions of Socrates, all the way into the twenty-first century. Even Plato's accounts are a seeming labyrinth of misdirection, as he makes Socrates the student of Parmenides, the disappointed reader of Anaximander, the initiate of a priestess of the Eleusynian mysteries, Diotima, and associates Socrates as well with Pythagorean and Orphic mystery religions. As Alcibiades puts it in Plato's *Symposium*:

> Socrates is unique; he is like no one else in the past and no one in the present – this is by far the most amazing thing about him. . . . [he] is so bizarre, his ways and his ideas are so unusual, that, search as you might, you'll never find anyone else, alive or dead, who's even remotely like him. The best you can do is not to compare him to anything human, but to liken him, as I do, to Silenus and the satyrs. (221c–d)

Plato leaves us with puzzles, some no doubt insoluble, when he broaches the topic of Socrates' lineage. In looking closely at Plato's own researches into Socrates, we uncover his attempts to chart Socrates' place within what we now call pre-Socratic philosophy. There is something as yet unexplained about the adumbration in Plato's *Parmenides* of Plato's theory of forms by a Socrates who (cf. Aristotle *Metaphysics* 1078b22–33) could not have been acquainted with it. The *Symposium*, *Parmenides* and *Phaedo* offer portraits of the young Socrates all of which deliver central tenets within a developing picture of the theory of forms.[1] Socrates is conceived as distancing himself from engagement with a particular teacher (Anaxagoras in the *Phaedo*'s 'intellectual autobiography of Socrates 96a6–100a7),[2] and in the *Charmides* and *Symposium* Plato suggests that, whatever the status of Socrates' preceptors, their wisdom comes from a source that is only provisionally human. As Socrates tells us in the *Apology*, he owes his profession in no small measure to the commands of the god, conveyed through 'oracles and dreams and in every way in which any man was ever commanded by the divine power' (33c). Plato also uses initiatory language and mythological settings, mystery religions and conventional Athenian state religion, to mention some but by no means all of the narrative resources at his disposal, to tell the story of Socrates' philosophical mission in the city of Athens. At times, Plato suggests that the preceptor of Socrates is a god: Asclepius (*Crito*: 'we owe a cock to Asclepius'), Apollo (*Apology*: 'I am in dire poverty because of my service to the god'), Artemis (*Theaetetus*: Artemis – 'the goddess of childbirth – is not a mother, and she honours those who are like herself'), Persphone (*Crito*: 'There came to me the likeness of a woman, fair and comely, clothed in white raiment, who called to me and said: O Socrates – The third day hence, to Phthia shalt thou go'), Zalmoxis (*Charmides*: the nature of the charm, which I learned when serving with the army from one of the physicians of the Thracian king Zalmoxis, who are said to be so skilful that they can even give immortality). In these texts Plato reveals that the methods that Socrates uses to practise philosophy and to develop in it are based on divine communications, on dreams, oracles, visions, possibly trances; at still other times, Plato makes Socrates pick up a book in the market-place, run into visiting philosophers, seek out poets, sophists, anyone who has anything to say about wisdom, including and perhaps above all his fellow citizens. The effect is to distance Socrates from his contemporaries, to put his wisdom slightly out of reach of ordinary human beings, to grant him access to worlds that are seemingly inaccessible in everyday life. Moreover, if we take all of the stories, legends and otherworldly visitations granted to Socrates within the narrative of Plato's dialogues, then it becomes difficult to confine our understanding of Socrates to his contributions to the history of logic or to see his work as confined to the tasks of pure reason alone.

When it comes to the reception of Socrates, the breadth of possible interpretations that we find in Plato is echoed variously as different epochs explore the meaning of Socrates' life: he is a proto-Christian martyr, a Sufi saint, an existentialist, a post-modern icon and many other things. Owing to the plethora of Socratic personae, we must by necessity be judicious. Here we treat Socrates' entrance into the modern world with Hegel's *Lectures on the History of Philosophy* (*LHP*), where the basics of the modern interpretation of Socrates are planted in seed form.[3]

HEGEL: SOCRATES BETWEEN *SINNLICHKEIT* AND *MORALITÄT*

We meet Socrates the individual, that is the philosopher who invents the philosophy of individualism, even of subjectivity, in the very first sentence of Hegel's chapter on Socrates in the *LHP*:

> Socrates is not only a highly important figure in the history of philosophy – the most interesting in the philosophy of antiquity – but he is also a world historical person. He is a major turning point of the spirit into itself; this turning represented itself in him, in his manner of thinking.

There is an odd conflation here between Socrates the unparalleled individual and Socrates the unparalleled philosopher of individuality who allows individual subjectivity to emerge full blown; here Socrates becomes a universal spokesperson for spirit, consciousness as such. It is as if previously the Greeks had focused on the what of existence; reality was conceived in terms of the priority of being or being in itself. After Socrates, the emphasis is on the who of existence; reality is conceived in terms of the priority of knowing:

> The Athenian poeple had come into a period of culture, in which this individual consciousness made itself independent of the spirit and became for itself. This was perceived by them in Socrates, but at the same it was felt that it meant ruin. (*LHP*, 447)

Hegel's Socrates is not as abstract as this celebrated pure consciousness would lead one to believe; he is at once profoundly political as well as ethical, or not only ethical, but the inventor of ethical philosophy, *Moralität*, which Hegel contrasts with *Sinnlichkeit*, with custom, tradition, convention. Hegel thus calls attention to Socrates' affinity with the Sophists, who as we saw constantly oppose *phusis*, nature, to convention, *nomos*, although Socrates offers us a way out of unreformed brutishness through the interventions of a self-consciously reflexive philosophy:

> the Socratic principle, the fact that what seems right and duty, good and useful to the subject in relation to himself as well as to the State, depends on his inward determination and choice. (*LHP* 448)

In this sense, Socrates opposes state and family, previous sources for ethics, and thus signals the already seeping erosion of *Sinnlichkeit*, presupposed by the Sophists.

> We now see Socrates bringing forward the opinion, that in these times everyone has to look out for his own morality, and thus he looked after his through consciousness and reflection regarding himself; for he sought the universal spirit . . . in his own consciousness. (*LHP* 409)

Not only does Socrates give us a philosophy of the individual self, then, but he does so because he is such a unique individual, an untimely hero who must become the first martyr for *Geist*:

> The principle of the Greek world was not yet capable of enduring the principle of subjective reflection; so it appeared as inimically destructive to it. Hence, the Athenian people were not only justified in reacting against it according to their laws, they were obliged to do so; they saw this principle as crime. That is the position of heroes in world history on the whole. (*LHP* 444)

A footnote on modern interpretations of Socrates would tell us that Hegel here develops a theme that infused the nineteenth and twentieth centuries, which is the likeness of the Socratic persona to either the tragic or the comic mask. Hegel's Socrates is decidedly tragic. As Most has written:

> Within Greek history it is for Hegel above all the trial and condemnation of Socrates which is most genuinely tragic, since Socrates represented a principle that could not help but come to expression, the freedom of thought which for Hegel is the motor of world history – but he represented it too early. (2007, 10)

Other modern philosophers saw more of the comic in Socrates, as perhaps Kierkegaard did; still others, including Nietzsche, saw Socrates as simply inimical to tragic art. Hegel's Socrates, then, invents something like the question that modern morality poses in a universal form, 'how should I act?' and, for the first time, thinks that this question can be settled through reflection on the question itself rather than by appealing to previously cherished normative values:

His philosophy, which asserts that real existence is in consciousness as a universal, is still not a properly speculative philosophy, but remained individual; yet the aim of his philosophy was that it should have a universal significance. Hence we have to speak of his own individual being, of his thoroughly noble character. (*LHP* 392)

Previously, according to Hegel, the principle of living for one's country or community served to shape the citizen's life:

Of the Greeks in the first and genuine form of their freedom, we may assert, that they had no conscience; the habit of living for their country without further reflection, was the principle dominant among them. (*LHP* 253)[4]

For White (2006) 'this outlook makes Hegel tend strongly to see philosophers and other thinkers as manifesting the workings in history of ideas that Hegel can treat as having a place within this teleologically shaped progression. The idea that's at work in a philosopher who's to be fitted into this scheme has to be the idea of freedom as Hegel construes it.' One additional strand of Hegel's philosophy shows up in the fabrication of our modern Socrates: not only is he the universal spirit coming into self-consciousness; he is, at the same time, an artfully crafted artefact of his own invention. The son of a sculptor, he sculpts himself:

resembling a perfect classical work of art which has brought itself to this height of perfection. Such individuals are not made, but have formed themselves into what they are; they have become that which they wished to be and are true to this. (*LHP* 391)

This description of Socrates as self-inventing is the basis of all modern interpretations of Socrates, far more so than his identity as inventor of morality. If one were to read these words in isolation, they might have been written by Nietzsche, Kierkegaard, Montaigne or even Nehamas; that they were written by Hegel, whose Socrates seems to be above all a universal expression of *Geist*, a shaper of the world, and also an agent and victim of its corruption, demonstrates how crucial Hegel is in the construction of the modern Socrates as a nexus of conflicting identities, the most individualistic of all individuals, the world-shaping author of universal law and the inventor of himself, whom later authors almost compulsively find themselves reinventing.

Now, Hegel's Socrates is not only the inventor of morality, the inventor of the individual, the inventor of conscience, the inventor of ethical philosophy; but he is also mainly critical, mainly negative and even destructive. He is the midwife of all kinds of philosophy, but in himself, he really just destroys others' views. How does he do this? First and foremost, he has a method. His method is deliberation itself; before Socrates, there was no deliberation – people acted according to the dictates of various authorities. After Socrates, people must deliberate because Socrates has destroyed authority. What we inherit from Hegel is a congeries: the self-inventor, the sceptic, the moralist, the strident individualist. All of this we meet again in Kierkegaard's Socrates.[5]

KIERKEGAARD: INFINITE IRONY

Kierkegaard's master's thesis,[6] on the *Concept of Irony with Constant Reference to Socrates*, famously takes up the Hegelian notion of Socratic irony and begins with an exaggeration of the negative side of Socrates that Hegel had already pointed to:

> irony [is] the infinite absolute negativity. It is negativity, because it only negates; it is infinite, because it does not negate this or that phenomenon; it is absolute, because that by virtue of which it negates is a higher something that still is not. The irony established nothing, because that which is to be established lies behind it.

It's obvious at once, upon opening this thesis, that Hegel's Socrates is very much the background for Kierkegaard's reading: Kierkegaard accepts that 'subjectivity makes its appearance for the first time in Socrates and that Socrates was essentially an enemy of traditional Greek culture. Influenced as I was by Hegel and whatever was modern, without the maturity really to comprehend greatness, I could not resist pointing out somewhere in my dissertation that it was a defect on the part of Socrates to disregard the whole and only consider numerically the individuals. What a Hegelian fool I was! It is precisely this that powerfully demonstrates what a great ethicist Socrates was' (*Journals*, X 3 A 477).

Socrates for Kierkegaard is the eccentric and idiosyncratic, caustic and catalysing ironist who, in the end, has nothing positive to offer. As a result, Kierkegaard's own version of Socrates might first appear to be strangely empty, as Kierkegaard himself readily admits. Were Socrates to meet John Climacus, the 'author' of Kierkegaard's pseudonymous *Philosophical Fragments*, then Socrates would admonish him and decry his motivations: 'My dear boy, you are a treacherous lover, for you are wanting to idolize me on account of my wisdom so that you would then be the one who understood me best' (6.27, quoted by Pattison 2007, 26). The idea, then, is that Kierkegaard must stand guard over Socrates' silence, lest he be convicted of appropriating Socrates; instead, Kierkegaard evidently will try to make Socrates appropriate him.

No doubt Kierkegaard's Socrates is someone who simply succeeds in being himself, an utterly unique individual who, in his very contingency, then, reminds the speculative philosopher of what he has forgotten. Life must be lived by individual human beings. Kierkegaard writes that on his epitaph he should like to see written, 'I was that individual [i.e. Socrates]'. At the end of his life Kierkegaard wrote an essay titled 'My Task' in which he tried to justify a life of writing and to reveal the mystery behind his own numerous masks (Kierkegaard most often wrote pseudonymously). 'The only analogy I have before me is Socrates; my task is a Socratic task, to audit the definition of what it is to be a Christian.'[7]

For Kierkegaard, this task is again not only one of *aporia*, denial, negation, but also one involving self-knowledge. He writes:

> Yes, I well know that it almost sounds like a kind of *lunacy* in this Christian world – where each and every one is Christian, where being a Christian is something that everyone naturally is – that there is someone who says of himself, 'I do not call myself a Christian', and someone whom Christianity occupies to the degree to which it occupies me.[8]

Kierkegaard's essay involves converting the text of the *Apology* into a living confrontation with his fellow citizens in Copenhagen, just as Epictetus' adaptation of the Socratic persona did not allow him to write treatises, but to confront the cadres of wealthy young men with the facts of their own inner contradictions, in light of their aspirations to be Stoics. Kierkegaard tries to make his fellow Christians aware of the ways that they fail fully to be Christian:

> I am not a Christian – and unfortunately I can make it manifest that the others are not either – indeed, even less than I, since they *imagine* themselves to be that or they falsely ascribe to themselves that they are that. (M340; SVI 14, 350–1)

Actually, Kierkegaard seems to leave it to Christianity and to the God of Christianity to provide a positive teaching. This topic lies almost outside the scope of our exploration, except to say that we would wrong to leave the impression that Kierkegaard's presentation of Socrates, for all of its valorization of the individual's conscience, the individual's love for his neighbour, and of Socrates as 'that individual', merely affirms the self, the desires of the self, and the situation of the self in the world. Nothing could be farther from Kierkegaard's depiction of Socratic practice than the eudaimonist's attempt to find his own good first and foremost. In fact, Kierkegaard hints that Socrates: In being adept at negation, was therefore adept at self-negation as well as world negation, or rather self-denial. The practice of Christian love paradoxically turns out to require something profoundly Socratic. In the same way, Socratic methodology has a place in the positive ethics of Christianity: it involves the seeker in a sustained thought, or even a single-minded thought, directed 'in self-deepening, so that one might discover the things that concern one's inner state, and such discovery is in the first instance very humbling' (*Works of Love*, 12.344, quoted by Pattison 2007, 31). In his *Upbuilding Discourse*, Kierkegaard evidently converts the thesis of eudaimonism, that everyone wants the good (i.e. for himself, above all) into its "counterpart: 'in order genuinely to will one thing, a man must genuinely will the good.' This willing the good is related to the Socratic insistence that everyone wants the good, and perhaps the subtlety here is that few indeed will the good. For this will entails that one 'must be willing to do all for it' or that one 'must be willing to suffer all for it'.

Kierkegaard's most extended Socratic meditation is the master's thesis, the writing that launched his career as a philosopher. In some ways it was an academic salute to Hegel's treatment of Socrates (a fact that Kierkegaard acknowledged when he wrote his previous work he played the part of 'an Hegelian fool'). The critical, negative, anti-dogmatic function of irony that Kierkegaard explores there is complemented, in Kierkegaard's lifelong engagement with the figure of Socrates, by positive interpretations that emphasize Socrates' contributions to philosophy. For example, we have seen that Kierkegaard interprets the Socratic 'maxim' 'everyone desires the good' in a way that equates it with single-mindedness, the willingness to suffer all for the good – that is, in a way that is directly inconsistent with eudaimonist interpretations that suggest that this Socratic doctrine refers to the agent's unalterable tendency to maximize his own happiness. Other examples of Kierkegaard's positive appropriation of Socrates can be found in his 'For Self-Examination', a treatise that starts by paraphrasing Plato's *Apology*.[9] The title itself, 'For Self-Examination', clearly speaks of the Socratic recommendation of self-knowledge, and the treatise begins with one of Kierkegaard's oblique references to Socrates as 'that simple wise man of antiquity'. Here Kierkegaard makes clear his relationship to Socrates when he continues, '[to whom] I nevertheless feel personally very indebted, and who lived in circumstances that in my opinion quite correspond to our situation today.' At times the treatise seems informed by *Alcibiades I*, as when Kierkegaard asks his reader to look into the mirror of self-examination and see God there. Compare *Alcibiades I*, lines 133c8–17, often excised on the grounds that they are spurious and that Plato somehow could not have written them:

> SOCRATES: Just as mirrors are clearer, purer, and brighter than the reflecting surface of the eye, isn't God both purer and brighter than the best part of our soul?
>
> ALCIBIADES: I would certainly think so, Socrates.
>
> SOCRATES: So the way that we can best see and know ourselves is to use the finest mirror available and look at God and, on the human level, the virtue of the soul.

Kierkegaard develops the theme of self-examination through an emphasis on inwardness, self-deepening and rational address that reflects a Socratic practice:

> It is precisely the turning of one's knowing inward toward oneself that makes one sober . . . that it therefore is by no means necessary to spend so much on developing one's knowing if only one sees to it that it takes an inward direction, ('Becoming Sober', 119)[10]

Kierkegaard again refers to Socrates obliquely in his 'Judge for Yourself', the companion piece to 'For Self-Examination', when he writes:

> Why should a person of conscience become angry if someone communicates something true to him! Indeed, he might rather become angry over the opposite. Say the following to yourself: is it an affront to treat a person not only as a rational being but as a person with a conscience to whom one tells the truth of the matter? (Preface, 90)

Kierkegaard here gathers a number of themes that illustrate how paradigmatic Socrates is, for what we have already seen is Kierkegaard's own task as a philosopher: his rational address to his reader, whom he asks to consider 'only himself', his truth telling as a form of enraging activity, and finally, like Socrates and Jesus, his self-humbling, which Kierkegaard 'likens to being nothing while calling attention to it'. That pointing to one's own nothingness is the activity of the philosopher in action. For Kierkegaard, all of this amounts to nothing more than being an individual, living one's life authentically: even his essay 'My Task', in some ways an apology for his own life of philosophy, reminds us that for 20 years he has been saying the same thing exactly as Socrates:

> What did Socrates' irony actually consist of? Could it be certain terms and turns of speech or such? No, these are mere trifles; maybe virtuosity in speaking ironically. Such things do not constitute a Socrates. No, his entire life was irony and consists of this: while the whole contemporary population . . . were absolutely sure that they were human beings and knew what it meant to be a human being, Socrates probed in depth (ironically) and busied himself with the problem: *what does it mean to be a human being?* By doing so he really expressed that all the bustle of these thousands was an illusion . . . Socrates doubted that a person was a human being at birth; it doesn't come so easy, and neither does the knowledge of what it means to be a human being.[11]

What we have discovered above all is the confusion that, as we saw, was present in the original sources between Socrates the individual and Socrates the paradigm, between Socratic philosophy (perhaps teaching?) and Socratic irony, between Socrates the critic of society and Socrates the criminal (for Kierkegaard, all of these things seem true of himself, of 'that individual'). The lifelong engagement with Socrates, coupled with the collapse of the distinction between life and philosophy, is what allows Kierkegaard to break free from the Hegelian interpretation of Socrates as subjectivity and to become a Socratic avatar. Bearing witness to one's own life and bearing witness to the soul of a people, the negative space that one must occupy for this work, becomes the Socratic persona transmitted in the modern age, not a positivist, discursive Socrates, but the very opposite. Anti-discursive, anti-dogmatic, individualistic and hardly more than an eccentricity – this is the tradition of Socrates as founding, paradoxically, a tradition that can never be a tradition.

An exception to the analytic, positivist style of Socratic scholarship represented by people such as Vlastos is to be found in a brilliant monograph by Alexander Nehamas, *The Art of Living* (1998). In it, Nehamas traces the Socratic tradition according to which life must be lived as the artistic creation of the individual. The *techne* analogy so often deployed in the elenctic dialogues must refer ultimately to the creation of a self, which of course cannot be merely the external product of one's wisdom, but must be that wisdom as it walks through life. For Nehamas, Socrates emits trace elements of both Hegel's and Kierkegaard's emphasis on radical subjectivity; the Socratic tradition thus culminates, as it were, in Foucault's *soici du soi*, care of the self (a philosophy that in turn relies on the Nietzschean project, which is a discussion of 'how one becomes what one is').[12] Nehamas reminds us that for Nietzsche, Cicero's Zopyrus story is a greater key to the personality and meaning of Socrates than the long pages of Platonic dialectic: 'When the physiognomist had revealed to Socrates who he was – a cave of bad appetites – the great master of irony let slip another word which is the key to his character. "This is true", he said, but I mastered them all.'[13]

NIETZSCHE: SOCRATES' ALTER EGO

Like Kierkegaard, Nietzsche, so to say, suffered or benefited from a lifelong engagement with Socrates, a relationship that in its own way has given rise to an entire interpretive tradition. Like Kierkegaard, too, Nietzsche casts Socrates as his protagonist in his first book;[14] for Nietzsche, Socrates ushers in the dawn of a new age, steeped in decadence, presupposing the corruption of values and loss of meaning that Socrates' presence both hastens and combats with a solution that brings with it a false consciousness. *The Birth of Tragedy* begins its treatment of Socrates with the typical emphasis on critical awareness that is the hallmark of the modern Socrates, his cerebral negativity: wherever 'Socratism directs its probing gaze, it sees lack of insight and the power of delusion, and it concludes from this lack that what exists is inwardly wrong and objectionable. Socrates believed that he was obliged to correct existence, starting from this single point; he the individual, the forerunner of a completely different culture, art, and morality, steps with a look of disrespect and superiority' (*BT* 66 Speirs trans.).

Nietzsche continues by calling Socrates 'the most questionable phenomenon' in Antiquity and asks, 'who is this individual who may dare to negate the nature of the Greeks?' (BT 13)

Nietzsche also apparently echoes Hegel's attention to the *daimonion*; for Hegel, Socrates appealed to the *daimonion* as an instantiation of a principle of reflection, according to which one should always act in such a way as the *daimonion* approves that is, the daimonion is a kind of personal universal. Nietzsche's *daimonion* is the instinct that obstructs instinct; it obscures life and is a monstrous demonstration of the aberrance of Socrates, who developed reason beyond its natural limits. Socrates exerted a powerful influence over Plato, who burned 'his poetry so that he could become a pupil of Socrates' (BT 13). And the Platonic dialogue became the new art form to replace tragedy, a form in which Socrates plays the part of the 'dialectical hero', who by his optimism drives tragedy away from the Dionysiac.

We have already seen that, according to Nehamas, in Socrates reason became a tyrant that allowed him to master his other desires, that 'cave of bad appetites', or instinct itself. Socrates silences poetry in favour of dialectic, and he also stifles desire as a whole: in *Daybreak*, without mentioning Socrates, but clearly with the anti-Socratic figures of Callicles and Thrasymachus very much in mind, Nietzsche writes that the pride of reason 'prevents us from having any sympathy with those vast stretches of the morality of custom' (*Daybreak*, BK.1 section 9), which we saw, according to Hegel under its label of *Sinnlichkeit*, fell victim to Socratic decadence.

Not everyone agrees that Nietzsche merely thinks that Socrates puts tragedy to death and silences poetry with the voice of reason. According to Porter (2000), what we see in Nietzsche much more resembles the dialectical play of opposing forces in Hegel. Whether the triumph of reason appears in Socrates as the death of tragedy, the denial of *Sinnlichkeit* and the establishment of morality as law-giving reason, or the domination of desire, appetite and instinct through rationality either as a form of self-creation or as legislation for the strong – all of it configures the Socratic persona as one end of the spectrum of Hellenism, as one of two opposing forces, both of which expand or contract in the vortex of culture at a given time, without ever converging. These forces are variously described as Dionysus and Apollo, Master and Slave, Reason and Instinct, and Tragedy and Dialectic. But also for Porter (2006), Socrates emerges not only as a symbol of his epoch, as master of life, in his guise as rational monstrosity, with his looming Cyclopean eye; he exists perhaps even more as a distinctly literary invention and inventor. Porter writes of a different kind of problem of Socrates from the ones we have so far studied, 'the circular problem that Socrates is as much an invention of literary tradition, and in particular of Plato, as he is the (unascertainable, unknowable) source of inspiration for that tradition' (2006, 413).

Conversely, Nehamas raises the question of whether Socrates' uniqueness is due to the creation of his student Plato's art, or whether it is due to his own art, which has been called the art of self-invention. If Nietzsche, like Montaigne and Socrates, is a philosopher of the art of living, then the problem will be one of originality. Nehamas considers that Socrates may have appealed to reason and aspired to universal truths that obtained for everyone, thus veering dangerously close to dogmatism. Yet, truth evaded Socrates, and he remained without the capacity to give law: reason's triumph instantly becomes reason's failure, which is why Nietzsche speaks of a Socrates become musical, and also why Nietzsche, according to Nehamas (1998), resents Socrates so very much. He is a paradigm whom no one can imitate, except those who, perhaps like Kierkegaard, and like Nietzsche himself, find themselves utterly alone, that is original. Others have contested this Socratic self-fashioning and found that it misrepresents the art that Nietzsche both practised and for which he took Socrates as his mentor. For Porter, once more, that work to which Nietzsche becomes apprenticed is a noble one, generous and magnanimous, fully devoted to life and not engaged in self-absorption: it is the art of soul searching. In describing and quoting Nietzsche's own description of Socrates' work, a work that Nietzsche has made his own, Porter allows us, finally, to see the benefit of our very search for Socrates. Is not this quest, in its own way, a search for 'that genius of the heart' that Nietzsche lauds, and whose touch must also change us who would discover him:

Anyone to whose task and practice it belongs to search souls will employ this very art *in many forms* in order to determine the ultimate value of a soul and the unalterable, innate order of rank to which it belongs. (ß263; trans. adapted; italics added)

Porter describes Nietzsche's task as a Socratic task, very much in the way that Kierkegaard assigned himself the Socratic task of being the only Christian, or rather being the only person who was not a Christian. Nietzsche, like Socrates, his mentor, is

the genius of the heart from whose touch everyone walks away richer . . . in himself, newer to himself than before, broken open, blown at and sounded out by a thawing wind, perhaps more unsure, tenderer, more fragile, more broken, but full of hopes that as yet have no name, full of new will and currents, full of new dissatisfaction and undertows. (ß295)[15]

In this chapter, we have seen that the modern Socrates was heralded as the initiator of an epoch in which private conscience took centre stage as the newly discovered voice of conscience which spoke out against both instinct and communal norms. We also saw that in modern analytic interpretations, Socratic philosophy is supposed to represent a psychological discovery, of psychological egoism, in which the individual agent considers his good and only his good; individual happiness alone becomes the criterion of rationality. Although the latter thesis has continued to attract scholarly approval and at times is granted the status of a truism whose truth does not have to be argued for, the former thesis, insofar as it can be attributed to Hegel, Kierkegaard and Nietzsche, is seen for the most part as an expression of a modern reading, not as a reflection on any actual 'philosophy of Socrates'.

FURTHER READING

Ahbel-Rappe, S. and Kamtekar, R. (eds.) 2006. *A Companion to Socrates.* London: Blackwell.

CHAPTER NINE

CITIZEN SOCRATES

If Hegel, Kierkegaard and Nietzsche all emphasized Socrates' authorization of individual conscience against the dictates of community and saw that, in the end, it was this authorization that led to his execution – the effective removal of that same conscience – then Continental philosophers of the twentieth century have emphasized the political implications of Socrates' fate. The postwar Socrates (post-World War II and post-Vietnam) emerges as a political theorist who represents the citizen's repudiation of the state's moral authority. Especially significant for defining the role of this citizen Socrates has been the work of three individuals: Hannah Arendt, Leo Strauss and Karl Popper – all of whom came to age under the brutal reign of Hitler, and all of whom suffered exile and expatriation. Not only did Socrates become an icon of individual conscience in the wake of the totalitarian regimes of Stalinist Russia and especially Nazi Germany, but, in another ironic twist of history, for Popper it was above all Plato's *Republic* and *Laws* that furnished the blueprints for these very regimes. In this chapter, we shall look at the work of these three thinkers and consider the extent to which Socrates has influenced modern political philosophy and, in turn, the extent to which politics has influenced the modern interpretation of Socrates.

CIVIL DISOBEDIENCE: THE *APOLOGY* AND THE *CRITO*

In order to frame the work of Arendt, Popper and Strauss, it will serve us well to review the *Apology* and the *Crito*. These dialogues treat the trial and imprisonment of Socrates. In the former, Socrates confronts and admonishes the representatives of the Athenian democracy, but in the latter he ultimately obeys the laws of Athens.

In brief compass, then, there is a controversy surrounding the consistency of these texts with respect to the political philosophy of Plato's Socrates. In the *Apology*, Socrates addresses his jury of 500 and – after explaining the nature of his philosophical activity, but before revealing himself as the city's unique benefactor, the gift of the god – poses a hypothetical question:

> If you said to me in this regard: Socrates, we do not believe Anytus now; we acquit you, but only on condition that you spend no more time on this investigation and do not practise philosophy, and if you are caught doing so you will die; if, as I say, you were to acquit me on those terms, I would say to you: Men of Athens, I am grateful and I am your friend, but I will obey the god rather than you, and as long as I draw breath and am able, I shall not cease to practice philosophy. (29c5–d6)

Socrates restates his resolve: I am not going to alter my conduct, not even if I have to die a hundred deaths (30c). Readers have long pointed to the apparent contradiction between the *Apology* and the *Crito*. The defiant statements in which Socrates makes clear that he would willingly 'disobey' the Athenians if they ordered his silence ('I will obey the god rather than you'), and the principle of obedience that Socrates enunciates in the *Crito* seem not to mesh. Here again Socrates imagines a hypothetical situation, in which the laws of Athens address Socrates, supposing that he follows Crito's urgings and unlawfully escapes from prison by bribing the jailer. Now Socrates hears the voices of the laws whispering in his ears their reproving disappointment: he can either obey the law or persuade those who make the laws to change them; he is not free to ignore them. The laws say:

> he has made an agreement with us that he will duly obey our commands; and he neither obeys them nor convinces us that our commands are wrong; and we do not rudely impose them, but give him the alternative of obeying or convincing us; that is what we offer and he does neither. (*Cr.* 51e8–52a2)

Does Socrates imply here, in this hypothetical exchange, that a citizen in a democracy who is granted the rights of redress, attending the assembly and expressing his views in communal deliberation, therefore has a duty to obey any and every law promulgated by that same democracy? Must he never disobey 'the commands' of the Athenian laws, and, if so, is he entitled to a 'Nuremberg defense'? Finally, how can these two distinct political perspectives, the one of open confrontation, or at least disobedience (with dutiful acceptance of the consequences, be it noted, up to and including death itself) and the other of complicity, or at the very least passivity, with regard to civil law, irrespective of its claims to justice, be consistent? This conflict itself becomes the foundation for a Socratically informed political philosophy of the twentieth century (although, in fact, Socratic civil disobedience was also invoked during the French Revolution, by Thoreau in the nineteenth century, as well as by civil rights leaders and anti-war protestors in the 1960s).[1]

Richard Kraut (*Socrates and the State*) devoted a monograph to the contradictions that appear between the *Apology* and the *Crito*, and, more recently, Dana Villa used the controversy to introduce a monograph on the political influence of Socrates (*Socratic Citizenship*). We can canvass several methods of reconciling what Villa has called, at the very least, the divergent tones of these two works that, dramatically speaking, are immediately connected. Some scholars see no contradiction between the defiance of the *Apology* and compliance of the *Crito*; according to this view, for Socrates all legitimate law must be obeyed. The Athenian jurists would have had no legal authority to demand silence in exchange for ignoring the charges brought against Socrates by Anytus, and, had they done so, they would not have been enacting a law but merely committing what is now called 'jury nullification'. In other words, we must take the *Crito* at face value and concur that Socrates might legitimately say, 'I was just following orders.' Therefore, Socrates is simply a legal positivist. For Kraut, on the other side, Socrates does not contradict himself in these two statements, both of which, let us remind ourselves, are couched as hypothetical, for the reason that the laws of Athens stipulate that citizens must abide by agreements that are binding because they are just: 'both in war and in the law courts and everywhere else you must do whatever your city and your country command, or else persuade them in accordance with justice' (51c quoted by Villa and explained by Kraut). Socrates has a duty to disobey whatever unjust laws he failed to have changed in public settings and to account for his disobedience in these same venues, by means of these same public institutions:

> if someone has disobeyed a law then he must, when summoned, appear before the court to persuade his fellow citizens that disobedience was justified. Persuasion is required of the disobedient citizen because he owes the parent city with which he has made an agreement some explanation for his behavior.

Nevertheless, Villa and others have criticized Kraut's ingenious attempt to reconcile the civil disobedience of the *Apology* with the implications of the *Crito*, which on the surface does demand complicity in laws that one finds unjust: 'both in war and in the law courts and everywhere else you must do whatever your city and your country command.' (*Cr.* 51c1) For Villa, Kraut ignores the urgency of the laws' demands on the loyalty of the individual as well as their self-described vulnerability when they are violated with impunity. As we saw in chapter three, Xenophon goes out of his way to portray Socrates as diligent in his obedience to the laws of Athens:

> But indeed with respect to justice and uprightness he not only made no secret of the opinion he held, but gave practical demonstration of it, both in private by his law-abiding and helpful behaviour to all, and in public by obeying the magistrates in all that the laws enjoined, whether in the life of the city or in military service, so that he was a pattern of loyalty to the rest of the world. (*Mem.* IV.4.1–14)

Xenophon's Socrates even goes so far as to bypass the Socratic *aporia* over the word justice, on which the entire plot of the *Republic* hangs, and simply equates justice with obedience to law:

> HIPPIAS: Now you are caught, Socrates, plainly trying to escape from a plain statement. When asked what you believe justice to be, you keep telling us not what the just man does, but what he does not do.

> Why, I thought for my part (answered Socrates) that the refusal to do wrong and injustice was a sufficient warrant in itself of righteousness and justice, but if you do not agree, see if this pleases you better: I assert that what is 'lawful' is 'just and righteous'.

Do you mean to assert (he asked) that lawful and just are synonymous terms?

SOCRATES: I do.

I ask (Hippias added), for I do not perceive what you mean by lawful, nor what you mean by just.

SOCRATES: You understand what is meant by laws of a city or state?

Yes (he answered).

SOCRATES: What do you take them to be?

HIPPIAS: The several enactments drawn up by the citizens or members of a state in agreement as to what things should be done or left undone.

Then I presume (Socrates continued) that a member of a state who regulates his life in accordance with these enactments will be law-abiding, while the transgressor of the same will be law-less?

Certainly (he answered).

SOCRATES: And I presume the law-loving citizen will do what is just and right, while the lawless man will do what is unjust and wrong?

HIPPIAS: Certainly.

SOCRATES: And I presume that he who does what is just is just, and he who does what is unjust is unjust?

HIPPIAS: Of course.

SOCRATES: It would appear, then, that the law-loving man is just, and the lawless unjust?

Contrast this picture of justice and law with Socrates' interrogation of Thrasymachus in *Republic* I (where Socrates raises the possibility of law-makers who err; presumably, erring in matters of justice, they would then promote unjust laws) and with what Socrates implies in the *Apology*, that all citizens, assembly, senate, jury, harm the young (presumably through inattention to human virtue), whereas Socrates himself does not do so. And the very verdict of the *Apology*, with its condemnation of Socrates, together with the enactment of his capital sentence, places Plato's version of Socrates firmly in contrast to the equation of law with justice. Later in the chapter, we shall consider

Strauss' interpretation of these passages from the *Memorabilia*, but for now we can note that, taken together, these passages bring up the question of obedience to law and its relationship to justice.

Both Plato and Xenophon cite Socrates' refusal to cooperate with the Thirty's orders: in Plato's *Apology*, Socrates tells us that the Thirty attempted to recruit him in the arrest and execution of Leon of Salamis (a distant relative of Socrates) as a part of their scheme for criminal self-enrichment. Xenophon tells a story about the Thirty prohibiting Socrates from practising philosophy by talking to the youths of Athens, which Socrates resists through elenctic refutation of the order.

The upshot is this: whether Socrates can be called a legal positivist or whether he represents, in Plato's dialogues, a notional confrontation with at least some unjust laws, historically he becomes associated with a tradition of civil disobedience: Martin Luther King Jr alludes to Socrates three times in his pamphlet 'Letter from a Birmingham Jail', defining civil disobedience (as opposed to anarchy) as the deliberate breaking of an unjust law and the willingness to pay the penalty for this violation. Listing Socrates among a long line of people who practised civil disobedience, including Jesus and the early Christians, in 'Love, Law and Disobedience' King compares the student activists of the civil rights movement to Socrates:

> This is what the students have followed in their movement. Of course there is nothing new about this; they feel that they are in good company and rightly so. We go back and read the *Apology* and *Crito* and you see Socrates practicing civil disobedience.

King's is perhaps one of the most famous of intellectual appeals to the figure of Socrates. Lane writes: 'In Plato's *Crito*, (49a–e) Socrates declares his loyalty to the principle that it is better to suffer injustice than to commit it. This moral standard appealed to the protesters against the war in Vietnam. It seemed to give them moral justification for opposing the commands of the federal government, in particular for resisting the draft and the punishments for draft-dodgers, and perhaps for protesting against the injustice of the war by breaking other laws' (Lane 2001, p. 29). Other scholars cite (merely) other scholars to show how interest in Socrates, especially the Socrates of the *Apology* and *Crito*, peaked in the 1960s; what remains iconic about King is his citation of Socrates as a part of his own defence of civil disobedience to ministers who asked him to practise restraint.

There is no definitive answer to the puzzles that the *Apology* and the *Crito* present, either over the question of Socrates' loyalty to the democracy as against the dictates of his own conscience or over the question of Socrates' attitude to the democracy generally. One point that emerges forcefully in Kraut's study, and is reiterated by the more recent work of Schofield (2006), is that Socrates' attitude in the *Crito* hinges on his endorsement of the mechanisms by which democratic *parrhesia*, freedom of speech, operates in Athens. In the *Apology*, Plato shows how Socrates relies on what we might today call the right to free speech when he speaks out against the illegal actions of the democratic government. Socrates happened to be the president of the assembly for a day (an office determined by lottery, not election) and opposed the assembly's motion to try a group of generals en masse, rather than individually as the law provided (*Ap.* 32b). More generally, his philosophizing in Athens is at least his own version of the public service that meant so much to democratic ideology. In the *Crito*, Plato allows Socrates to pay homage to the laws of Athens, conceding that, after all, Socrates himself has benefited from the democratic laws of Athens, the city in which he has practised his lifelong mission.

Although it is Socrates' identity as an Athenian that grants him access to this *parrhesia*, we have seen that the Socratic schools celebrate what then becomes a tradition of philosophical 'speaking truth to power'. One thinks of the Diogenes–Alexander anecdotes: once Alexander the Great chanced to come upon Diogenes sunning himself and asked whether there was any favour he might do for him. Diogenes replied: 'Yes: Stand out of my sunlight' (D. L. vi, 38). The tradition is continued in the discourses of Epictetus, many of which discuss how the sage will treat with Caesar, with high officials, what the office of the free person is and who counts as free. Epictetus, the former slave, was in the habit of addressing his students as 'slave', and his discussion of political freedom trades on the study of inner autonomy, the integrity practised by the Stoic or philosopher who wills only one thing, virtue. In the treatise titled 'How Should We Be Disposed towards Tyrants?' Epictetus invokes the inner freedom that is the result of the sage's *apatheia*, his indifference towards all that is not truly his own:

It is not possible for that which is by nature free to be disturbed or impeded by anything except itself. Judgments are what troubles a person. For when the tyrant tells someone:

I will chain your leg.

The man who sets high value on his leg says:

No; pity me.

Whereas the man who sets high value on his rational choice says; if that seems to you more profitable, chain it.

You don't care?

I don't care.

I will show you that I am master.

How can you? Zeus has liberated me. Do you suppose that he was likely to enslave his own son? But you are master of my corpse; take it.

You mean that when you approach me, you don't attend to me.

No I attend to myself. But if you want me to say that I attend to you too, I tell you that I do so in the way that I attend to my water jug. (Quoted by Long 2002, 197)

Epictetus understands Socratic politics fundamentally as the art of self-rule; this practice of self-possession frees Socrates (and his imitators) from coming under the power of others. Xenophon commends Socrates' behaviour in his trial, not begging for mercy or pleading for his life, exactly on these grounds.

If Socrates is unwilling to play politics in the courtroom and use emotional persuasion to influence the judges even though the stakes are so high, and if he is unwilling to participate in outright acts of murder under the auspices of common thugs, that does not make him an outspoken opponent of Athenian imperialism at its brutal nadir. In fact, Socrates makes clear in his trial that he has avoided politics as usual in the city of Athens:

Be sure, men of Athens, that if I had long ago attempted to take part in politics, I should have died long ago, and benefited neither you nor myself. Do not be angry with me for speaking the truth; no man will survive who genuinely opposes you or any other crowd and prevents the occurrence of many unjust and illegal happenings in the city. A man who really fights for justice must lead a private, not a public life if he is to survive for even a short time. (*Ap.* 31d5–32a2)

The tradition of Socrates as promoting frank speech against tyrants and despising life itself in comparison with virtue does not quite entitle one to attribute an explicit political philosophy to Socrates, to call him a political philosopher or even the first political philosopher. However, it might be argued independently of any modern interpretations that the *Apology* is simply about Socrates' political philosophy and his complex engagement with Athenian democracy. Therefore, the political Socrates is no modern innovation; rather, Socratic politics are the very impetus for Socratic literature, and are entirely presupposed by it. It may seem incredible that Greek scholars would take the trouble to criticize the politics of a philosopher who lived almost 2,500 years ago, yet Greek professors who came of age in the 1960s and witnessed the mass protests of the civil rights movement and later demonstrations against Vietnam have criticized Socrates for being in fact apolitical. Athens invaded Syracuse in 415 BCE, a catastrophic venture that decimated Athens; Athens also committed atrocities, including the murder of civilians, women and children, against the island of Melos. Why, if Socrates constantly champions justice, as Plato maintains in the *Apology*, would he not speak up in the assembly against these crimes? For Vlastos,[2] speaking on the campus of the University of California, Berkeley, the site of so much activism, Socrates' explanation in the *Apology* amounts to a poor excuse. He writes:

the defeatism of this retrospective judgment is unwarranted; why discount the effect of cool sardonic comment from Athens' gadfly to bring down a degree or two the overheated atmosphere of the debate? Would it not have been [Socrates'] duty to do whatever he could, little or much, to make the voice of reason heard, regardless of consequence to himself? (129)

Part of the reason for this intensified scrutiny of Socratic politics and Socrates' possible *Gleischschaltung* (adjustment to policy – the word Arendt used for intellectual accommodation to Nazi policy during the 1930s) was the extreme interest that this topic held for political philosophers who theorized the Greeks in the aftermath of exile from

Germany and of the Holocaust.[3] When it comes to Socrates, others have defended him here, again of course in retrospect, but taking as their cue something we have already had occasion to mention, the way that Plato distances Socrates from the stance of the simple *apragmon*, the politically inactive man, and instead goes out of his way to stamp Socrates with the title 'busybody' (*polupragmon*), someone who refuses to 'take it easy'.[4] For example, Lane (2000) cites *Gorgias* 521d6–e2:

> I believe that I'm one of the few Athenians – so as not to say I'm the only one, but the only one among our contemporaries, to take up the true political craft and practice the true politics. This is because the speeches I make on each occasion do not aim at gratification but at what's best. They don't aim at what's most pleasant. And because I'm not willing to do those clever things you recommend, I won't know what to say in court.

People have defended Socrates on the grounds that, unlike the many worried classics professors who condemn him, Socrates actually did address generals, arms dealers, and political leaders face to face, and used his philosophy to dispense 'advice' [*sumbouleuein*, a word used in the assembly of one addressing the crowd].

In what follows, we shall see how modern readings of Socrates by political philosophers make Socrates precisely into a political philosopher.

ARENDT: PUBLIC DISCOURSE, PRIVATE VICE

Hannah Arendt begins her essay 'Philosophy and Politics' with a reference to the *Apology*:

> The gulf between philosophy and politics opened historically with the trial and condemnation of Socrates, which in the history of political thought plays the same role of a turning point that the trial and condemnation of Jesus play in the history of religion. (Arendt 1990, 57, originally a lecture delivered at the University of Notre Dame)

For Arendt, to continue, the condemnation of Socrates 'made Plato despair of polis life and, at the same time, doubt certain fundamentals of Socrates' teachings' (57). Socrates' death was an object lesson to Plato, convincing him of the very points he makes so forcefully in the *Gorgias* and in the *Apology*: persuading the crowd differs significantly from persuading an individual. In the future, Plato would work against the democratic endorsement of persuasive speech and set up a tyranny of truth whose authority undercut opinion. According to Arendt:

> To Socrates, as to his fellow citizens, *doxa* was the formulation in speech of what *dokei moi*, that is, of what appears to me. This *doxa* had as its topic . . . the world as it opens itself to me. It was not, therefore, subjective fantasy and arbitrariness, but also not something absolute and valid for all. The assumption was that the world opens up differently to every man, according to his position in it. (Quoted by Villa 2001, 265[5])

Everyone has his or her part, so to speak, in creating what might be thought of as a public fiction, in the sense not that it is utterly false, but that it is a co-invention of all of the inhabitants of the public sphere. The more adept these people are at truth-telling and the more articulate they are in formulating their views, the better they become qua citizens: 'the role of the philosopher then is . . . not to tell philosophical truths but to make the citizens more truthful', says Arendt in 'Philosophy and Politics' (quoted by Villa 2001, 262).

The Socrates of Arendt's 'Philosophy and Politics' emerges from a sympathetic reading of the *Apology* and the *Gorgias*, according to which the examined life, the life of self-reflection, is the requisite for, perhaps not an enlightened society, but at the very least a more thoughtful, questioning citizenry. That this attitude of questioning, self-reflection and even doubt is political is shown in Arendt's 'Eichmann in Jerusalem', where Arendt considers the role of Socrates as gadfly, as awakener from the slumber of convention. If Socrates in 'Philosophy and Politics' served as the midwife to help people see something of the truth in themselves, primarily by allowing them time away from the sphere of the public fiction, in 'Thinking and Moral Considerations' Arendt focuses on the contamination of this very public world by convention, habit and the tendency to cleave to prescribed rules of conduct. In this essay, Arendt reflects on her observations of the Nazi war criminal Adolf Eichmann at his trial in Jerusalem. She writes:

> This total absence of thinking attracted my interest. Is evil-doing, not just the sins of omissions but the sins of commissions, possible

in the absence of not merely 'base motives' as the law calls it but of any motives at all, any particular prompting of interest or volition? . . . Do the inability to think and a disastrous failure of what we commonly call conscience coincide? The question that imposed itself was: could the activity of thinking as such, the habit of examining and reflecting on whatever comes to pass . . . could this activity be of such a nature that it conditions men against evil doing? (Arendt 1990, 51, nos 1–2, 8 quoted by Villa 2001, 265)

Socrates' activity as a thinker, not a knower, is as one who questions but does not teach, who gets people talking and weans them away from the claptrap of convention by sitting with them, alone, and helping them to bring forth what is within, or else Socretes confronts them in their somnambulism and, waking them up, freezes them in their tracks with the sting of thought – either way, Socrates is political qua thinker, and the public sphere as such is a product of thought. There is no politics without thought. It is in this sense that Socrates is a political philosopher, much more so than Plato, who seemed rather to embrace politics and wrote several dialogues explicitly dedicated to statecraft. Arendt's compatriots Leo Strauss and Karl Popper also developed their meditations on political philosophy both in response to the totalitarianism of Nazi Germany and as students of Socrates and Plato.

STRAUSS: THE CITY AND THE PHILOSOPHER AT ODDS

For Leo Strauss, arguably a much more conservative thinker than either Arendt or Vlastos, Plato becomes assimilated to Socrates covertly, while outwardly differing from his teacher in openly espousing political theory and even insisting that 'until philosophers are rulers' there can be no justice in the city. Time and again Strauss turns to the topic of Platonic political philosophy, which ultimately reverts to Socratic political philosophy. What Strauss means by this must now be examined. In *The City and the Man*, in an essay called 'On Plato's *Republic*', Strauss writes: 'philosophy and the city tend away from one another in opposite directions' (*CM*, p. 125). Although Strauss often speaks of the philosophical aspiration towards knowledge, as opposed to mere opinion, and in this sense assimilates Socrates to Plato, in fact Strauss rejects the Arendtian understanding of Plato's 'tyranny of reason'. In much of his work, including *The City and the Man*, *Persecution and the Art of Writing* and *Platonic*

Political Philosophy, Strauss explores this fundamental opposition of the city and the philosopher, exemplified by the Athenian hostility to Socrates, in whom they were correct to see elitist tendencies. Even so, the aspiration to wisdom is not the same as the attainment of wisdom. Therefore, Plato's metaphysical strictures on hisphilosopher-rulers, the requirement that the philosopher-ruler have a vision of the form of the good before he assumes his mantle of public service, are ironic. The theoretical life by its nature rejects dogmatic formulations. And for this very reason, the philosopher is useless to the city, which must rely on a partisan ascription of priority to a given position, which, being temporal, is to some extent arbitrary and contingent. Strauss writes:

> Socrates makes clear in the *Republic* of what character the city would have to be in order to satisfy the highest need of man. By letting us see that the city constructed in accordance with this requirement is not possible, he lets us see the essential limits, the nature of the city. (*CM* 134)

Straussian interpretations of the *Republic* and of Plato as a whole stress the ironic, non-disclosing nature of the text and tend to read dogmatic, or even doctrinal, pronouncements with the assumption that Plato wrote for two audiences: those who can appreciate the force that Socratic *aporia* and doubt about the ultimate truthfulness that merely human institutions carry without thereby becoming disillusioned about what ultimately is of value, which is truth for its own sake, and those who belong firmly in the realm of the city and value only its accoutrements.

Strauss' Socrates, for all of his irony, is not apolitical, however. His philosophy is not political in the sense that Arendt's Socrates cultivates the politics of self-reflection in the city, following, as we saw, Plato's *Gorgias*. His message, that the good itself consists in seeking wisdom, valorizes the contemplative life absolutely. Strauss' Socrates knows 'the first lesson' of politics, which is precisely that philosophy is not for the masses; that is why Socrates is represented in Plato as talking only to the elite and why Xenophon distinguishes between two kinds of Socratic listeners: those with Socratically approved qualifications and those who counted themselves as among his circle but were actually not fully initiated. Nevertheless, Socratic political philosophy is not a political doctrine, for the reason that, as we saw, it merely recommends that the philosopher not become entangled with the affairs of the city and, therefore, that the philosopher lead the life of the *apragmon*: the private man who more or less withdraws from active participation in civic life in order to pursue a form of good that can never be approximated, approached or made known in the political arena of the public fiction. In this sense, Strauss' Socrates might be at odds with Plato's own portrait of the *Apology*'s 'busybody' who actively intervenes, not so much in the affairs of the city as in the lives of those who conduct these affairs.

Strauss, in Villa's words, posits a 'counter-intuitive' reading of the *Republic* as a critique of political ideology and, indeed, of the very attempt to reform the polis as the site of a possibly ideal regime which opens the possibility of the true good, philosophical life, to its citizens. The examined life that Socrates recommends is the best life, but this life should not and cannot be brokered to the masses through the force of persuasion, and certainly not imposed upon them by the elite through the mechanisms of a totalitarian or even utopian state. Strauss' political response to Socrates, as someone to warn against the excesses of elevating the political at the expense of the spiritual or intellectual, has often been embraced as a positive call to conservatism, on the one hand, and to precisely the kind of power brokering and elite manipulation or concealment of the truth, on the other, that one sometimes sees among statesmen who claim to be his followers. But this 'neoconservative' endorsement of Strauss, which assumes the existence of a virtuous few who can and should extend their influence through the amassing of enormous power, is the very antithesis of Strauss' endorsement of Socratic moderation and contemplative virtue.[6]

POPULIST SOCRATES VERSUS ELITE PLATO: KARL POPPER

Perhaps no interpretation of Platonic political philosophy could be more at odds with Strauss' ironic reading of the *Republic* than that of Karl Popper,[7] the Austrian-born author of *The Open Society and Its Enemies*, whose second volume is titled, ominously, 'The Spell of Plato'. Popper wrote the book while in exile in New Zealand and in a preface to the second edition proclaimed that he began the book the day that he received news of the German invasion of Austria in March 1938. As our subject is Socrates, and Plato only insofar as it is necessary, as it frequently is in understanding

Socrates, to invoke Plato, Popper's condemnation of the *Republic* and *Laws* as a blueprint for the totalitarian and racist Nazi regime will occupy us only briefly. Popper writes: 'because of his radical collectivism, Plato is not even interested in those problems which men usually call the problems of justice, that is to say, in the impartial weighing of the contesting claims of individuals. Nor is he interested in adjusting the individual's claims to those of the state. For the individual is altogether inferior. "I legislate with a view to what is best or the whole state", says Plato' (106). What we are more interested in is the etiology that Popper presents for Plato's rigid caste system, rooted in what Popper calls 'racialism', and supported by a system of educational ossification, in which people who are 'too old to think independently' presumably will gratefully accept full initiation into the cohort of dogmatists whose chief intellectual task will be to indoctrinate the next generation of philosopher-rulers (133).

For Popper, the greatest invention of the Greeks was the 'open society', the artificially constructed public realm that depended on the competition for standing, independent of one's tribal affiliation. Open societies operate in terms of what Popper calls 'abstract relationships' such as exchange or political cooperation; individual initiative fuels these relationships. Socrates, then, is the philosophical patron of the individualism already catalysed in democratic Athens but requiring a champion to tame the excesses of its power politics (191). Thus Socrates, at heart friendly to the democracy, is mistakenly taken as its enemy, an assumption that is disproved by his loyal submission to the laws of Athens in the *Crito* and, of course, historically, through his choice of execution rather than exile (194). Popper ends his book by showing the great contrast between Socratic free thinking and criticism of authority and political institutions and Plato's 'theory of inquisition', coolly and carefully elaborated in Plato's *Laws*.

SOCRATES THE COSMOPOLITAN

Our survey of these three thinkers and their widely disparate articulations of the meaning of Socratic political philosophy has revealed obvious continuities with modernist readings of Socrates in general, particularly Hegel's association of Socrates with individual conscience (a belief that prompted him to think that Socrates fully deserved his death at the hands of the Athenians, however tragic this exigency proved to be). Today, Strauss is widely influential and represents a strain of Platonic interpretation that veers away both from Popper's much more literal reading of the text and from the analytic analysis of texts that characterizes most Anglo-American Plato criticism.

When studying the politics of Plato's Socrates, we must be aware of the history of reading Plato in history and of the way that the continued reading of Plato's dialogues shaped the history of philosophy. Although scholars have found plenty in the words of Socrates and Plato to fuel both anger and admiration, perhaps we should, after this survey, let Plato's Socrates have the last word. First, let us recall that Socrates characterizes his own work as political: 'I believe that I'm one of the few Athenians . . . to take up the true political craft' (*Gor.* 521d). Yet, apart from specific requests the Athenians made for Socrates' services – at Potidaia, as *epistates* of the *boule* – Socrates avoided politics as usual. In what sense, then, is his philosophical practice the work of a citizen or political? Brown, to cite one example, finds that it is precisely in Book I of the *Republic* that Socrates is made to articulate a philosophy of global citizenship, when he argues against Polemarchus that 'it is the function not of the just person to harm either a friend or anyone else, but of his opposite, the unjust person' (335d11). At a minimum, the just person has the obligation to any and every human being, regardless of their status as friend or enemy, not to harm them.[8] In our age of globalism, we might, then, make Socrates the first global citizen.

FURTHER READING

Brickhouse, T. and Smith, N. 2002. *The Trial and Execution of Socrates.* Oxford: Oxford University Press.

Lane, M. 2007. 'Gadfly in God's Own Country: Socrates in 20th Century America', in M. Trapp, ed. *Socrates in the Nineteenth and Twentieth Centuries.* London: Ashgate. An important article on the politics of Socrates.

Monoson, S. 2000. *Plato's Democratic Entanglements.* Princeton, NJ: Princeton University Press.

Schofield, M. 2006. *Founders of Modern Thought: Plato.* Oxford: Oxford University Press. Contains a good account of the politics of Socrates as well.

Stone, I. F. 1989. *The Trial of Socrates.* New York: Anchor.

CHAPTER TEN

CONCLUSION: SOCRATES AND SELF-KNOWLEDGE

KNOW THYSELF

All of the interpretations we have considered so far, be they modern or ancient, sceptical or dogmatic, political or philosophical, have tended to focus in one way or another on the questions surrounding Socrates' disavowal of knowledge and the extent to which Socrates constitutes himself as a teacher, has teachings or doctrines, and is sincere or ironic in his denial that he has any wisdom, great or small (*Ap.* 21b). Nevertheless, there is one approach to Socrates not yet explored here in any depth, and it may allow us to make progress on some of the perplexities we still face. In the final analysis, we must go back to the beginning of Socratic literature, and to the profound meaning of the encounter with Socrates as first and foremost an interview that seeks to reveal the person behind the role, ambition, reputation, opinion – in short, to reveal the person behind his or her *doxa*. Socrates above all aims to help inculcate self-knowledge in his interlocutors. It is this knowledge that, it turns out, will be the knowledge requisite for virtue and this knowledge that, since it can belong only to the person who comes to know himself or herself, cannot be transmitted by Socrates to another, and with respect to which Socrates' own possession of knowledge of virtue is not a pre-requisite. We have seen hints of the importance of self-knowledge emerge in various strands of interpretation: Kierkegaard mentions the process of 'self-deepening'; Nietzsche writes movingly of Socrates as 'the genius of the heart from whose touch everyone walks away richer . . . in himself, newer to himself than before' (*BT* 295, quoted by Porter 2006, p. 425); Arendt speaks of Socratic solitude and inner dialogue as the ground of civic discourse. And, of course, Plato and other Socratic writers place self-knowledge and the Delphic injunction 'Know thyself' at the heart of several key Socratic dialogues.

Six dialogues[1] – two elenctic dialogues, two dialogues that feature what one might call Socratic moments in a kind of diptych with the rest of the dialogue, and two whose dating and authenticity present greater problems – provide us with evidence that the elenchus is primarily intended to elicit self-knowledge and that Plato consciously links the character Socrates with this theme. Five of these dialogues, *Apology, Charmides, Theaetetus, Phaedrus* and *Alcibiades I*, emphasize Socrates' connection to Delphi and to the precept 'Know thyself' either through direct allusion to Delphi or through mention of a divine patron who sponsors Socrates' activity.

THE DELPHIC ORACLE IN THE *APOLOGY*

In the *Apology*, Socrates' chief witness for the defence is Apollo. Of course, the specific testimony to which he alludes during the trial is the oracular dispensation to the effect that 'no one is wiser than Socrates', but it is clear that Socrates associates this response with the Delphic precept "Know thyself". Socrates interprets the statement 'no one is wiser than Socrates' at 23b1 to mean 'whoever realizes, as Socrates does, that he has in reality no worth with respect to wisdom is wisest among you.' This interpretation amounts to the admission that Socrates in fact possesses self-knowledge in at least this respect, that he knows he has no wisdom.

It is evident that Socrates' interpretation of the oracle is dependent upon his possessing this self-knowledge, since he falls into a state of perplexity when confronted with the oracle precisely because he knows he has no wisdom.[2] This perplexity marks his self-admission that he has no knowledge, but at the same time it helps him to recognize the value of his self-knowledge. By means of the oracle, Socrates comes to believe that it is the distinctive mark of one who possesses wisdom to know that he has no wisdom. That is, Socrates becomes the delegate of the Delphic injunction 'Know thyself', extending both his own self-inquiry and his peculiar brand of wisdom to his successive interlocutors. That the elenchus is his recommended method for self-inquiry is supported by the fact that the most important procedural requirement for the elenchus is that the respondent say what he believes to be true. The Socratic interview aims at self-knowledge even as it relies upon self-knowledge for its continued operation.

What is the connection between elenctic procedure, the requirement that the interlocutor say what he believes to be true, and the final goal of the elenchus, knowledge of virtue? The traditional interpretation of the elenchus as the search for moral knowledge seems overly ambitious; how can the elenchus prove or disprove a given thesis? The most it can do is to show that within the context of a certain belief set the thesis must be rejected, not because it is false, but because it is inconsistent with a given interlocutor's other beliefs. However, Socrates' reliance upon the elenchus seems anything but ambitious: how certain can it be that the elenchus will ever advance our moral knowledge?[3]

Socrates reflects back to the interlocutor what the interlocutor shows to Socrates. A Socratic encounter is, so to speak, a confrontation with the self, by the self. This interpretation of the elenchus does not make of Socrates a dogmatic teacher of any kind, nor does it impute to him a set of beliefs that he either holds to be true or invariably discovers that his successive interlocutors hold to be true. For the conclusion of the elenchus will not be simply a proposition descriptive of what the interlocutor knows or does not know, nor will it be simply a state of belief, whether that state be true or false. In fact, this interpretation does not make of Socrates a moral teacher in the sense that he wishes to impart or to discover moral tenets. If we are to take Socrates at his word when he claims to have no knowledge of virtue,[4] then there is a strong temptation to follow Socrates' own strategy when he shows that, without such knowledge, moral instruction is mere pretense.

Perhaps we can begin to see why Socrates might have found it worth his while to engage in the elenchus with others, whether or not their opinions might assist him in his own search. Since the elenchus is a process of continually refining one's self-inquiry, Socrates makes sure that any answers obtained during the course of it do not displace the living reality of the person who makes the inquiry. There is no reason to think that Socrates cannot promote virtue, even if he lacks definitional knowledge of virtue. In fact, virtue is not a matter for definition at all; as self-knowledge, it relies on a practice. The practice is that of the examined life. Since Socrates is not a dogmatic teacher, Socratic opinions cannot be parroted successfully; he must, if presented with formulaic Socratic answers, continue past them to a seeming impasse.

Socrates, to engage in the elenchus, does not have to have any special definitional knowledge of virtue. What is required for its success is knowledge of oneself as knower. But Socrates cannot give this knowledge to another in the form of a definition; he can only point to its operation in practice, that is, in the elenchus, which is just the practice of self-inquiry. In beginning to receive the benefits of the Socratic elenchus, one must undergo a kind of reversal. Rather than looking outward at the objects of desire or forward to the fruits of action, the learner is asked to redirect attention inward, towards his state of mind. It is this readjusted orientation to life rather than any doctrinal system that Socrates seeks above all to inculcate by means of elenctic practice. As Socrates puts it:

> I do nothing else besides go around trying to persuade the young and old among you alike not to be attached to your bodies nor to your possessions nor to anything except to the effort to make your souls as virtuous as possible. (*Ap.* 30a7–b1)

What remains to be accounted for is the relationship between the kind of definitional knowledge that Socrates is apparently seeking and the self-knowledge that seems to accrue at the expense of the former. If it is self-knowledge and not definitional knowledge that enables one to become virtuous, then why does Socrates expend so much effort in trying to distil moral definitions? In part, I have already answered the question by suggesting that it is just the aporetic realization that virtue cannot be defined but only lived that the elenchus is designed to bring about. Nevertheless, as they stand, the texts apparently show that Socrates considers a certain kind of objective knowledge to be requisite for virtue.

VIRTUE AS SELF-KNOWLEDGE VERSUS VIRTUE AS KNOWLEDGE OF THE GOOD

In the Socratic dialogues, the theme that virtue is knowledge underwrites Socratic intellectualism. In the *Laches*, Nicias' definition of bravery is 'knowledge of things terrible and confidence inspiring' (194e11–195a1). At *Gorgias* 460b9, Socrates gets Gorgias to agree to the inference 'he who has learned justice is just.' Again, in the *Meno*

(89a4), Socrates says that 'virtue, either in whole or in part, is wisdom.' Generally in the dialogues Socrates fills out the conception of virtue as knowledge by alluding to a 'science of good and evil', or 'science of the advantageous'. In the *Charmides* we are presented with two competing versions of the Socratic formula: virtue is self-knowledge and virtue is knowledge of the good; a last-ditch effort to reconcile them fails. Perhaps we should have expected as much: the exponential ambition of this projected science of the good seems out of keeping with the equally ubiquitous ignorance that Socrates professes. It seems doubtful that Socrates embraces this science of utility as a serious enterprise. For one thing it sits poorly with the disavowal of knowledge (*Apology*, *Lysis*, *Laches*), and it is also the subject of an internal critique in the very dialogues in which it is espoused. In the *Charmides*, Socrates shows us two flaws with Critias' epistemocracy: successful action does not necessarily make us happy (*Ch.* 173d6), nor is wisdom, qua wisdom and not qua craft, to be valued for its utility (175d2).

In the case of the Socratic theses – no one errs willingly; it is better to suffer than to commit injustice; virtue benefits the one who possesses it; virtue is knowledge – several explanations for this feature of unanimity or the uncontested assertion of these theses in a Socratic conversation are proffered in the literature. Most scholars agree that Socrates avers the truth of these precepts at least partially on the grounds that they remain undefeated in elenctic arguments. Furthermore, Socrates thinks that all people will agree to these same precepts, given time to reflect on them and despite their initial protestations to the contrary. Why is it that these precepts alone arise from the elenchus as indefeasible moral truths?

While Socrates' interlocutors nearly always defer to Socrates' brand of virtue-centred eudaimonism, experience confirms that conflicts between virtue and self-interest are inevitable. Scholars have tried to explain the compliance of Socrates' interlocutors in several ways. Irwin has suggested that, in the end, Socrates must rely on the self-evidence of the proposition that virtue always benefits the person who possesses it.[5] Brickhouse and Smith, following Vlastos, suggest that for success in the elenchus, Socrates relies upon a latent but universally held belief system that equates with his own views.[6] Other writers, such as Robert Bolton and Raphael Wolf, emphasize the derivation of the elenchus from logical foundations. The self-evidence, for example, of the principle of non-contradiction is the logical structure from which the pragmatic goals of the elenchus – that is, clarifying the belief structure of the interlocutor and removing contradictory beliefs – are derived.

But whether we emphasize the substantive contents of a supposed Socratic belief system or we emphasize the importance of dialectical principles in the conduct of the elenchus, the status of the Socratic theses can probably never be determined with accuracy. Are they advanced as hypotheses, presented as dogmas, subject to retraction, survivors of previous elenchi? We can't actually know. Instead, we can look to their deployment within the Socratic conversations and notice the work they do in situ. Do the Socratic theses, which certainly function as the dialectical engines of the elenchus, have any pragmatic functions; is their dialectical value related to an ethical component?

Of course, the answer to this question is yes. Both the procedural requirements of the elenchus, that the interlocutor say what he thinks is true, and the subject matter of Socrates' conversations, in which participants articulate their deepest, or core, values, guarantee that the resulting discussion involves a high degree of self-disclosure on the part of the interlocutor. Although it is common to see the elenchus as a kind of covert inculcation of a moral system, in fact the elenchus itself often results in emotional reactions of anger (Thrasymachus, Anytus, Meletus),[7] narcissistic grandiosity (Euthyphro, Hippias),[8] profound ambivalence (Alcibiades), sadistic rage (Callicles) or neurotic dullness (Laches). Very few of Socrates' patients noticeably improve, and even if the Socratic thesis survives the elenchus, it seems clear that its deployment has revealed deep pockets of resistance in the psyches of Socrates' conversational partners.

Therefore, a dynamic, interpersonal dimension of the elenchus includes the emotional shortcomings of its practitioners, as they fail to meet the requisite ethical challenges or demands on character that Socrates makes of his interlocutors. Likewise, for the interlocutors, as is the case with Clitophon, there is a sense in which Socrates fails to meet the importunities or perhaps actual needs of his interlocutors. We saw that Clitophon endured his frustrations with Socrates, wondering why the other could not teach him 'the path to happiness through virtue'. Clitophon represents a typical interlocutor, one endowed with a kind of minimal philosophical curiosity, but who tends to become discouraged and feels bogged down by an evident lack of progress. Yet, far from envisaging later, Platonic psychology as a correction of the psychological naïveté of Socratic intellectualism, ironically we might see the failure of a Socratic ethics as crucial for its successful deployment.

So one aspect of the elenchus is a self-disclosure that permits the interlocutor to step outside of an ordinary subjectivity and to view this subjectivity from another perspective. This peculiarly moral emotion is one of the practical pivots of the elenchus. As Socrates tells us in the *Theaetetus*, most of his students are ready to bite him when he deprives them of some pet folly. The emotional energy that is invested in the interlocutor's response charges the elenchus, turning it into a profound and sometimes shattering encounter. Asked to disown his desires, the interlocutor then encounters his own affective states very much as if they belonged to another. In the *Apology*, for example, Socrates asks his interlocutors to examine their ordinary and conventional desires for such things as wealth or fame (29e1). Even though the experience of *aidos* or shame originates in a rather conventional disapproval of the person one has become, the interlocutor is not meant to become the victim of Socratic humiliation.

Despite Socrates' insistence, according to the prudential maxim, that everyone desires the good, at least as revealed within the work of the elenchus, most desires, not to say virtually all of his interlocutors' desires, are precisely for what is not good. People seem concerned with getting ahead in life, or just getting on with life, with advancing their place at the expense of others, and many contemplate actions and desires that truly occasion revulsion. Even those who actually evince the occasional desire for virtue (Clitophon, Alcibiades) or instruction more generally (Laches) are actually half-hearted about this desire. In fact, we saw that one of the initial functions of the elenchus was the hard work of instilling the desire for virtue, or for the good, into the interlocutor.

Thus, much of the work that the elenchus does will be to help the interlocutor discriminate among his own desires, or, rather, among his affective states in general. During the elenchus habits of thought, emotional reactions and entrenched opinions all come to the surface. In the *Hippias Major*, when Socrates asks Hippias about *to kalon*, Hippias reveals his fondness for pretty women, fine horses and lots of money (288a ff.). These attachments indicate something about the structure of Hippias' personal desires as well as about the locus of value in the community to which he belongs. But once he articulates these values, the elenchus offers Hippias a forum in which to question their authenticity. Why does Hippias think horses are so wonderful? Isn't a cooking pot just as beautiful in its own humble way? This very encounter with Socrates authorizes but does not necessarily promote a certain amount of detachment from his passions, states of mind and desires, and allows Hippias to notice their contingency, both cultural and personal. In other words, the fact that one has a desire does not in and of itself countenance the belief that one ought to fulfil it. Moreover, the fact that one has a belief does not in and of itself warrant that one hold it, and the fact that one is in any particular state of mind does not warrant that one persist in that state of mind.[9] Often Socrates encounters his interlocutors on the verge of doing something rash, such as Euthyphro's prosecution of his own father on charges of homicide appears to be, or such as persisting in a complacent, self-assured state of mind that is based on the need to rush into action to secure, precisely, the object of one's desire. It is in this sense that Socrates speaks of *sophrosune* in the *Charmides* as knowledge of knowledge, that is, as awareness of what one represents to oneself.

The elenchus relies on and functions in concert with the cultivation of self-knowledge, and it is ultimately the ability to discern the knower, to discriminate the knower from any of the *doxai* that it happens to know, that constitutes the basis of the freedom that Socrates invokes in the elenctic situation, as we saw.

At *Charmides* 174d5, Critias tries to advance the argument that if *sophrosune* is knowledge of knowledge, then it will be beneficial by governing other kinds of knowledge, including knowledge of the good. Socrates counters by asserting that only productive knowledge can be beneficial. Thus Socrates brings his examination of *sophrosune* to an end by explicitly criticizing the definition of self-knowledge as knowledge of knowledge, on the grounds that he has discovered it to be useless:

> We granted that [*sophrosune*] was knowledge of knowledge, although the argument refused to allow it and even denied it. And to this knowledge we granted the knowledge of the productions governed by the other knowledges, even though the argument would not allow this either, in order that our temperate person might know that he knows what he knows, and that he does not know what he does not know. (175b6)

The upshot is that Socrates will admit that, in the end, knowledge of knowledge cannot be a worthwhile pursuit, at least in terms of the utility it might provide:

> I am very sorry on your behalf, Charmides, if you with your looks and your great modesty will enjoy no benefit from this temperance, nor will its presence in your life assist you. (175e1)

There is knowledge that leads to successful action and there is knowledge of the self. Knowledge of knowledge seems to be a candidate for rejection as a definition of temperance because it affords no utility to the one who possesses it. Knowing what one knows, the virtue of temperance, is not, it turns out, expert knowledge that allows one to examine another's claims to expertise, nor is it expertise in the science of happiness that allows one to control more or most situations. Socratic knowledge asks its interlocutors to develop from controlling others (using expertise on them) to controlling (knowing) oneself, from fighting with weapons to caring about truth. In making this transition, the interlocutor catches what one might call a glimpse of the knower. Alcibiades' words from the *Symposium* hint at this look within:

> I don't know whether anybody else has ever opened him up when he's been being serious, and seen the little images inside, but I saw them once, and they looked so godlike, so golden, so beautiful and so utterly amazing. (216e4)

It is now that we can appreciate Socrates' advocacy of self-knowledge as virtue and as knowledge of the good. The virtues, the adornments of wisdom, are to be discovered in the knowing self – bravery, temperance, piety, wisdom and justice. Socrates' search for the definition of virtue, in the sense of the disposition of the virtuous person, ends in the qualities that attend the knower. In bringing forth the mind that seeks wisdom and truth, that attends to desire and aversion, pleasure and pain, indeed to any object of thought however great or small, the person with self-knowledge, that is the person who knows himself or herself to be primarily a knower, finds what Socrates refers to as 'guardian temperance'. We are now in a better position to understand some of the puzzles left unanswered in the previous chapters.

For example, Socrates suggests in the *Protagoras*, as we have seen, that virtues are one. Perhaps the sense of this suggestion is that virtue, as self-knowledge, allows the person to become brave by becoming aware of fear, temperate by becoming aware of desire or aversion, and just by becoming aware of the state of mind, the inner disposition, of, say, *pleonexia*, which might fuel injustice.

Again, we are in a better position to understand why virtue might be knowledge, though not a craft or a science – that is, its aim is not to produce anything. Finally, we now can better see why, if virtue is self-knowledge, Socrates does not necessarily agree with the Sophistic position that virtue is teachable. Above all, the links between virtue and self-knowledge explain the overwhelming presence of Delphi and the Delphic precept in Plato's Socratic dialogues.

THE *THEAETETUS* AND SOCRATIC MIDWIFERY:
A PSYCHOANALYTIC APPROACH?

One of the results of Vlastos' developmental hypothesis was, as we saw, the tendency to separate off the elenctic dialogues as representing the philosophy of the historical Socrates from the 'later' dialogues, in which, again in the terms of developmentalism, Socrates somehow is supposed to function merely as a 'mouthpiece' for Plato. And yet the *Theaetetus*, chronologically late, continues the theme of Socrates and self-knowledge developed in the *Charmides*, *Apology* and *Alcibiades I*. Here Socrates once more returns to the familiar disavowal of knowledge and of wisdom. The topic of conversation, the object of the 'what is X?' question that Socrates raises with his interlocutor, Theaetetus, is of immense scope: Socrates asks Theaetetus, 'what is knowledge?' The theme of the dialogue is a direct reflection on the meaning of Socrates' own disavowal of knowledge. According to one persuasive interpretation,[10] in the *Theaetetus* we see Plato engaged in a reprise of the Socratic method, looking back at Socrates and asking how Plato's own philosophy is related to it. The answer is partly given in the form of a telling metaphor that Socrates in the early part of the dialogue uses to describe his philosophical activity: he is a midwife (149a). This is Socrates' account of his duties as a philosophical midwife (150b7–d1):

> Now my art of midwifery is just like [that of ordinary midwives] in most respects. The difference is that I attend men and not women,

and that I watch over the labor of their souls, not of their bodies. And the most important thing about my art is the ability to apply all possible tests to the offspring, to determine whether the young mind is being delivered of a phantom, that is, an error, or a fertile truth. For one thing I have in common with the ordinary midwives is that I myself am barren of wisdom. The common reproach is that I am always asking questions of other people but never express my own views about anything, because there is no wisdom in me and that is true enough. And the reason of it is this, that God compels me to attend the travail of others, but has forbidden me to procreate. So that I am not in any sense a wise man; I cannot claim as the child of my own soul any discovery worth the name of wisdom.

For Sedley not only is this passage a compelling summary of Socrates' activity as a philosopher, primarily helping his interlocutors to achieve self-knowledge under the auspices of a goddess (in this case, Artemis, but we have also seen her twin brother, Apollo, undertaking the same function in the *Apology* and elsewhere), but it is also a reminder about Plato's own relationship to his teacher: in some sense, Socrates is the midwife of Platonism. Hence, the Socratic emphasis on self-knowledge becomes the Platonic doctrine of knowledge as recollection. From the earliest Socratic dialogues to the last, Socrates is portrayed as the great mirror for the soul. We have already met one of the more colourful Socratic interlocutors (a favourite of Nietzsche and one not even found in the Platonic corpus): a physiognomer with the name of Zopyrus who comes into town and purports to read human souls by looking at people's faces.[11] Recently, the trained psychoanalyst and philosopher Jonathan Lear has written an article pointing to the affinities (not necessarily historical, although Freud was an ardent reader of the Greeks in general and Plato in particular) between psychoanalytic technique and Socratic method. In his essay 'Socratic Method and Psychoanalysis', Lear asks, 'Can conversation make a fundamental difference to how people live? Socrates is thought to have been trying to improve the lives of those he talked to, through his peculiar form of conversation' (p. 442). In this question lies a strong argument for the meaning of Socratic irony. According to Lear, 'Socratic irony is not a turn of phrase but a way of life. It is made possible by a peculiar gap between pretense and aspiration that is embedded in our lives' (p. 455). Lear owes more than a little to

Kierkegaard's and Nehamas' conceptions of an ironic life, rather than mere ironic speech. Socrates points to the distance between *doxa* and reality, which we have seen over and again in this study.

Lear writes:

> the whole contemporary population can be sure they are human. In their lives, their professions, their social roles they put themselves forward *as* human. Call this the *pretense* of the concept in the literal, non-pejorative sense of 'the putting forth of a claim.' There need be no hypocrisy involved. The members of the contemporary population in the very living of their lives *put forward a claim* that this is what is involved in living a human life. But the concept also has an aspiration which typically transcends the social practice. We glimpse this when we ask, of a particular act, was that a *humane* thing to do? The question is not about whether the act was perpetrated by a member of the human species. Or if, at university, we consider the division of the *humanities*: by and large the division teaches remarkable aspects of the human spirit.

THE *ALCIBIADES* AND SELF-EXAMINATION

I want to close this chapter and this book by looking at a test case of aspiration. It is the case of the young Alcibiades, a man on the threshold of his political career, a man who is full of aspiration, who is almost entirely aspiration. The question posed by Socrates is: 'are you ready to be a leader in Athens?' This is certainly what Alcibiades claims; it is, to use Lear's words, his pretense. Let us listen to the interview between Alcibiades and Dr Socrates.

When Socrates' *daimon* finally allows him to speak to Alcibiades, the latter is no longer a teenager, but has already grown a beard and is about to embark on his life's ambitions. Not content to be a leading man in Athens, Alcibiades thinks that ruling the world, being master of all men, sounds like a good job description (*Alcibiades I*, 105). But Socrates is not so sure that Alcibiades has the qualifications: compare yourself to the kings of Persia, Socrates urges. Don't you know how they are raised from early childhood? After they have spent seven years with select and highly prized eunuchs, their education is overseen by four great sages possessing the four cardinal virtues of moderation, wisdom, courage and justice. The wisest among them teaches the young prince the wizardry that belongs to Zoroaster, son of Ohoromazda, and teaches as well the royal art, the art of ruling oneself (*Alcibiades I*, 122a2).

But this same art, the art of ruling oneself, is just what Socrates is going to teach the young Alcibiades to prepare him for his career goals, to be master of the universe. How does one rule oneself? First, Alcibiades needs to know himself. He should take care lest he end up knowing what is his, but not himself. Here Socrates distinguishes between what is oneself and what belongs to oneself:

> SOCRATES: The art by means of which we each care for our self is different from the art by which we attend to what belongs to our self?
>
> ALCIBIADES: Apparently.
>
> SOCRATES: There, when you are attending to what belongs to yourself, are you attending to yourself?
>
> ALCIBIADES: By no means.
>
> SOCRATES: Therefore, it is not the same art, evidently, the art by which one could care for oneself and the art by which one can care for one's possessions.

We return to the exhortation to wisdom found in the *Apology*: this care for the soul, how it may be as good as possible, is care for the self as a knower, as knowing and only knowing is the proper function of the human soul. In the *Charmides* (165 ff.) Socrates asks whether there is an intentional state that is not about anything other than itself, that forms its own object. Is there a seeing *not* of this or that, but a seeing of the seer? A knowing not of this or that, but a knowing of that which knows? Yes, there is, though no one in the *Charmides* admits it. Yet Socrates demonstrates it in the elenchus. But if so, it is not an object at all. This is the paradox: to be the knower is something active, alive, an activity. It is not a thing that is known. This is the living virtue of wisdom that Socrates talks about in the *Alcibiades*.

ENCOUNTERING SOCRATES, ENCOUNTERING ONESELF

What we can take away from our encounter with Socrates, then, is both distress and some degree of reassurance. The distress arises because it is all too easy to see how little solidity there is in the views of those who would like to develop a full-blown theory of elenctic epistemology, Socratic ethics based on egoistic eudaimonism, or even a theory of how to read Plato's dialogues in such a way as to yield a figure who we can claim resembles the historical Socrates. We have also seen how many thinkers, far from giving us a picture of Socratic philosophy, have used the Socratic invitation to self-knowledge as a way to insert their own philosophical projects or have inserted Socrates into a history of philosophy that is of their own making. What reassurances, then, can we find in this study of Socrates that any of our perplexity can be allayed? Rather, it is because our encounter with Socrates has left our perplexity intact that we can be sure we have not transgressed beyond the boundary of Socratic wisdom into thinking that we know what we do not. And thus we are decidedly better off.

NOTES

CHAPTER ONE: SOCRATES: THE MAN AND THE MYTH

[1] Cf. Nails 2002 under *Socrates* for a judicious treatment of the facts.

[2] Cf. Phillips 2001. Phillips, a former journalist, describes his adventures bringing what he calls Socratic philosophy and his own interpretation of the elenchus to participants all over the United States in a variety of venues. Cf. also Marinoff 1999, a best-selling self-help manual that touched off the explosion of the technique of 'philosophical counselling' in the United States.

[3] For an overview of Socrates scholarship from Winkelmann and Schleiermacher to the late Professor Vlastos, see Ausland 2006.

[4] Kahn 1996; Clay 1994.

[5] Mostly available in Giannantoni's monumental 1990 collection *Socratis et Socraticorum Reliquiae*.

[6] Nevertheless, even those who embrace this now increasingly discredited view of the so-called Socratic dialogues must also add the finely wrought portraits of Socrates found in the *Symposium* (Socrates' initiation into the mysteries of love at the hands of the priestess Diotima and Socrates' composure in battle at Potidaia), *Theaetetus* (Socrates' self-description as a philosophical midwife), and of course *Phaedo* (Socrates' execution in prison).

[7] Vlastos 1991, 1994.

[8] Vander Waerdt 1994.

[9] See Vander Waerdt 1994, passim, and also Long 2006, 8–10. Long discusses the figure of Socrates as presenting the Greeks with a new understanding of virtue as self-control. *Enkratiea*, the Greek word meaning 'self-mastery', is the essential characteristic of the Socratic paradigm, according to Long, as we discover Socrates in both Xenophon's and Plato's dialogues. Moreover, it is the appeal of Socrates as possessing inner power and strength that accounts for the popular impact of Socrates on Hellenistic ethics (for which see chapter six below).

[10] For Aristotelian texts on Socrates see 'The Evidence of Aristotle and Xenophon' in Vlastos 1991. Vlastos cites *Meta.* 1078b16–17, where Aristotle summarizes Socrates' contributions to the history of Greek

philosophy as 'occupying himself with the moral virtues having been the first to search for universal definitions of them' (Vlastos 1991, 91). On virtue as knowledge see *Magna Moralia* 1182a15–18: 'Coming afterwards, Socrates spoke better and more fully about [virtue]. But neither did he speak correctly. For he made the virtues forms of knowledge and this is impossible.'

[11] There are Cynic and Stoic technical vocabularies that, as we shall see below, attempt to capture some of the features that Socrates exhibits in his life: one example is the Cynic word *Karteria*, which denotes endurance, fortitude, an attitude and capacity for toughness. The Cynics and Stoics identified this virtue with what they read or heard about Socrates' exemplary toughness, as when he is reported to have walked barefoot through the Thracian winter snows (*Symp.* 220b).

[12] For this point, see Most 1993.

[13] McLean 2007, 65.

[14] Sedley 2004.

[15] From the *Charmides*, we learn that Socrates met a doctor from Thrace while he was stationed at Potidaia: 'Well Charmides, it is just the same with this charm. I learned it while I was with the army, from one of the Thracian doctors of Zalmoxis, who are also said to make men immortal' (Sprague 1962, 156d).

[16] 'I don't know if any of you have seen him when he's really serious. But I once caught him when he was open like Silenus' statues, and I had a glimpse of the figures he keeps hidden within: they were so godlike' (216e; Nehamas and Woodruff 1997).

CHAPTER TWO: THE LIFE AND DEATH OF SOCRATES

[1] In my discussion of Plato's works and how they relate the events of the trial, I follow Nails 2006.

[2] Diogenes reports that this version of the indictment against Socrates is the verbatim wording of the formal charges that a second-century-BCE witness, Favorinus, claims he read in the public archives of Athens, stored in the Metroon, a temple in which the Athenians deposited their public documents.

[3] It is difficult to compare modern and ancient currency, but one way to think about the value of a *mina* is to say that it is equal to 100 drachmas, where a drachma is the standard wage for a day's labour. So Socrates offers the equivalent of ten years' labour of accumulated wealth. Thus, it turns out to be a significant amount of money.

[4] Nails 2006.

[5] Cf. Pucci 2002.

[6] The exact date of this alleged pamphlet is disputed. Xenophon actually does not name Polycrates; instead, he uses the collocation 'the prosecutor says'. One of the few sources for the name Polycrates is very late, found in a declamation of Libanius, a rhetor of the second century BCE. Some doubt the existence of such a pamphlet altogether.

[7] Janko 2006.
[8] Edwards 2007, 127.
[9] Alon 1995, 2006.
[10] Wilson 2007; Mainz 2007.
[11] Goulbourne quotes *The Complete Works of Voltaire*. (Oxford: Voltaire Foundation, 1968–), 114: 337.
[12] Indeed, the subject of Socrates' death was set for the Royal Academy's Grand Prix in 1753 (Mainz 2007, 251).
[13] Mainz 2007, 249. Cf. also Lapatin 2006; Wilson 2007.

CHAPTER THREE: THE SOURCES FOR SOCRATES

[1] Dorion 2003; Waterfield 1999.
[2] Cf. Vander Waerdt "Socrates in the Clouds" 1994 and Nussbaum (1980).
[3] Kerferd 1981; Woodruff 2006.
[4] Antiphon fragment 44c, *On Truth*, Pendrick 2002, 186–7.
[5] Cf. Weiss 2006 on Socrates' ad hoc purveying of Sophistic theses for the sake of winning an argument. In this case, it is precisely the Gorgianic thesis that Socrates evidently embraces, though his doctrinal commitment is at issue for Weiss.
[6] For the fragments of *Phaedo*, we must rely on the edition of Rossetti.
[7] For this account of Antisthenes, I rely on Prince 2006 and suggest themes I develop more systematically in Rappe 2000.
[8] Although Plato mentions him only once by name, in fact some of Antisthenes' work is thought to inform the *Theaetetus*. Cf. Burnyeat 1990.
[9] Another follower, Aristippus, is said to have founded the Cyrenaic school of philosophy. Cf. Tsouna-McKirahan 1998.
[10] ἀλλ' ἐν πενίᾳ μυρίᾳ εἰμὶ διὰ τὴν τοῦ θεοῦ λατρείαν.
[11] This is not to deny that Antisthenes himself wrote theoretical works and investigated topics that were strictly outside of the purview of ethics. In fact, we have quite a few lengthy fragments from his writings as well as good indications in his theory of reference. But as they perhaps take us rather far from our topic, which is the status of the Socratic writings vis-à-vis their value as witnesses to Socratic philosophy, we must forgo discussion of these areas of Antisthenes' philosophy. See Brancacci 1990; Caizzi 1966.
[12] *SSR* fragments 43–54. See Giannantoni 1990a, 2: 609–10; Denyer 2001, 1–29. Cf. O'Connor 1994; Kahn 1996.
[13] *SSR* fragment 53.
[14] Kahn 1996; Rossetti for the fragments of Phaedo's Socratic dialogues, missing from *SSR* as Kahn notes. Cicero actually mentions the *Zopyrus* twice in his own work. Kahn rightly emphasizes other important Socratic themes present in the fragment: the notions of practice, of moral self-improvement and of care of the soul.
[15] 'Ethical Philosophical Power' in Long 2006 From Epicurus to Epictetus: studies in Hellenistic philosophy. Oxford: Clarendon Press.
[16] Plato *Apology* 19d and 33a.
[17] O'Connor 1994, 170.

[18] On this episode see Morrison 1994, whose account I follow here.

[19] Stevens 1994; Strauss 1970.

CHAPTER FOUR: PLATO'S SOCRATES

[1] Perhaps to these we might add a fourth, agnostic, a position that makes no assumptions one way or the other about the relationship between Plato and Socrates, and assumes that at any point in the dialogues, Socratic teaching might or might not be invoked.

[2] Nevertheless, Vlastos' framework was largely anticipated by Zeller and the work of nineteenth-century philology.

[3] Vlastos 1991, 47–9.

[4] In alphabetical order, *Apology, Charmides, Crito, Gorgias, Hippias Minor, Ion, Laches, Protagoras, Republic* I.

[5] *Republic* II–X, *Phaedo, Phaedrus, Symposium*, at the very least.

[6] Cf. Nails 2000.

[7] Here I follow the account of Kahn 1996, and especially Kahn 2002.

[8] Kahn 1996; Nails 2000.

[9] Nails, private correspondence to the author.

[10] Adkins 1960, *Merit and Responsibility* 30–60, cited by Ausland 2002, 37, n. 4.

[11] Ausland 2002, 37. The more technical later use of the masculine noun *elegchos* is to be understood accordingly in forensic context, where it refers more narrowly to refuting the claims of an antagonist by testing them or putting them to the proof.

[12] Vlastos 1991.

[13] Nehamas 1998.

[14] Vlastos' crucial article on the method of the elenchus and its positive results, 'The Socratic Elenchus', is found in Vlastos 1994.

[15] For these questions see Kraut 2006.

[16] Here I mean primarily Kahn 1996.

[17] This language is employed by Blondell 2002.

CHAPTER FIVE: SOCRATIC METHOD AND EPISTEMOLOGY

[1] In Greek some of the words that Socrates uses to describe his own activity are *exetasis, elegnchos, logos*, and *dialegesthai*. Cf. Tarrant 2002.

[2] On the priority of definition see 'Meno's Paradox and Socrates as a Teacher' and 'Socratic Intellectualism' in Nehamas 1999. See also Beversluis 2000.

[3] Beversluis 2000, 108, summarizing Geach, with whom he emphatically disagrees. Beversluis goes on to show in this article that Socrates everywhere accepts examples of courage and even provides his own examples.

[4] Cf. Bett 2002 and chapter two above for a brief discussion of Sophistic ethics. Plato explores the epistemology of the Sophist Protagoras in the *Theaetetus*, 166a–168, and his human-measure hypothesis, according to

which each human being has a valid perspective, seeing things as they are in relationship to himself or herself.

5 Irwin 1995, 69.
6 Cf. also the following passages:

T2. *Protagoras*, 358d1:

> No one willingly goes to meet evil or what he thinks to be evil. To make for what one believes to be evil, instead of making for the good, is not, it seems, in human nature, and when faced with the choice of two evils no one will choose the greater when he might choose the less.

T3. *Meno*, 77e1:

> Isn't it clear then that this class, who don't recognize evils for what they are, don't desire evil but what they think is good, though in fact it is evil; those who through ignorance mistake bad things for good obviously desire the good?

> For them I suppose that is true.

> Now as for those whom you speak of as desiring evils in the belief that they do harm to their possessor, these presumably know they will be injured by them?

> MENO: They must.

> SOCRATES: And don't they believe that whoever is injured is, in so far as he is injured, unhappy?

> MENO: That too they must believe.

> SOCRATES: And unfortunate?

> MENO: Yes.

> SOCRATES: Well, does anybody want to be unhappy and unfortunate?

> MENO: I suppose not.

> SOCRATES: Then if no, nobody desires what is evil, for what else is unhappiness but desiring evil things and getting them.

T4. *Euthydemus*, 278e4:

> Do we all wish to do well in the world? Or perhaps this is one of the questions which I feared you might laugh at, for it is foolish, no doubt, even to ask such things. Who in the world does not wish to do well?

> Not a single one, said Clinias.

[7] On the procedural requirement that Socrates is only interested in statements that the interlocutor holds to be true, and its relationship to the elenchus as a genuine quest for truth, see Vlastos 1991, 140: 'Since Socrates' real purpose is not merely to search out and destroy his interlocutor's conceit of knowledge, but also to advance the search for truth, if he is to find it by this method, while professing to know nothing, he must worm it out of them.' See also Benson 1992, 63–4; 2000.

[8] In chapter six below we shall explore the topic of eudaimonism – an ethics that posits happiness (Grk. *eudaimonia*) as the goal of all action

[9] Vlastos 1983.

[10] Tarrant 2006 writes: 'Of the Platonic passages used by Vlastos as testimonia T4, T5, T8, T15, T17–18 and T20–4 (477e–8a, 472c–d, 500b, 473e, 472b–c, 479e, 472b, 474a, 474b and 482a–b) derive from the *Gorgias*, with T20 (479e) and T24 (482a–c) playing especially important roles. The later pages play an even greater role in Vlastos' 1985 account of Socratic knowledge, including T6 (509a), T9 (505e), T12 (486e), T16 (512b) and crucially T28–30 (508e–9a, 479e, 505e–6a).'

[11] Tarrant 2006.

CHAPTER SIX: HAPPINESS AND VIRTUE

[1] A traditional genre of philosophical literature that aims at converting someone to philosophy.

[2] Reshotko 2006 refers to these neutral or indifferent things, a class that actually includes most things, as NGNB: neither-good-nor-bad. See Penner and Rowe 2005 for a discussion of our passage, *Lysis* 219.

[3] In mentioning the Aristotelian use of en*doxa*, I certainly do not wish to dismiss the central argument of the *NE*, the specification of a complete end for the sake of which we do everything, as mere en*doxa*.

[4] The strongest proponent of this interpretation remains Vlastos 1991: virtue is a principal, but not the only, thing desirable for its own sake. As Vlastos explains (217), virtue, remaining the invariant and sovereign good, would of itself assure a sufficiency of happiness.

[5] For instrumentalist interpretations of Socratic ethics, cf. Irwin 1995, 73–5. For another strong defence of the instrumentalist interpretation, see Reshotko 2006, chapter 5. Happiness is the only unconditional good and it is the only self-generated good. According to Reshotko, virtue is an unconditional good, but it is other-generated (it is valuable only because it leads to happiness).

[6] Examples of this approach include Reshotko 2006, Vlastos 1991, and Penner and Rowe 2005. A notable exception to this interpretation may be found in Weiss 2006.

[7] Vlastos, 'Happiness and Virtue' n. 14, in Vlastos 1991.

[8] Reshotko's discussion of the neither-good-nor-bad is salutary; cf. Reshotko 2006, chapter 5.

[9] Cf. Irwin 1995, section 25, 36–8.

[10] Cf. Weiss 2006, 85–93. Weiss locates the fallacy by means of which Socrates gains Polus' agreement in a sleight of hand by which Socrates easily

substitutes morally loaded words for the morally neutral words that Polus employs in his axiology.

[11] *Gorgias* 477b5: 'Do you consider there is an evil condition of the soul? And do you call this injustice and ignorance and cowardice and the like?'

CHAPTER SEVEN: THE SOCRATIC SCHOOLS

[1] Previously scholars emphasized the Stoic hostility to Plato, and saw in their embrace of Socrates a self-conscious attempt to repudiate Plato and claim they were Socratics. Most scholars today appreciate the influence of Plato's dialogues and philosophy as a whole on Stoicism.

[2] *Dissertationes* 3.24.67 = *SSR* VB 22.

[3] Long 2002, 69, quotes this and discusses the place of Socrates in the thought and methods of Epictetus.

[4] Cf. Long 1996b who discusses the relationship between this passage in Plato and the Stoic theory of value, as well as the Cynic idea of perfect indifference as an ethical goal.

[5] Margaret Graver's 2002 translation and commentary on the *Tusculan Disputations* has ample material to clarify the history of Stoic psychology. See also Sorabji 2000, 29–120.

[6] Long 1971, 1989.

[7] See Long 1988.

[8] Long 2002, chapter 2.

[9] Cf. Long 2002, 27–31.

[10] For a technical discussion of the faculty of assent, see Inwood 1985.

[11] Long's translation, 2000, 142.

[12] See Sorabji 2000, 30, who cites the following primary texts: Cicero *TD* 4.11–22; DL vii.110–14; Ps.-Andronicus *On Emotions* 1–5 = *SVF* 3.391, 397, 401, 409, 414.

[13] Brittain 2006 has translated this book as *Cicero on Academic Scepticism*. For a discussion of the history Cicero presents in this partially extant work, see Brittain's 2001 monograph.

[14] For this view of Arcesilaus see Long 2006.

[15] On Socratic and Stoic paradoxes see Brown 2006.

[16] Quoted and translated by Long 2002, 85; cf. Long 2002, 70.

[17] Here I follow the account of Riley 1980.

[18] Frischer 1982.

[19] For the texts of these two treatises by Philodemus, *On Frank Speech* and *On Vices*, see Konston et al.; Teubner 1911.

CHAPTER EIGHT: SOCRATES IN THE MODERN WORLD

[1] Cf. Linck 2007.

[2] On Socrates' historical and intellectual associations with contemporaries, see Janko 2004. See also Linck 2007.

[3] In this section of the chapter, I follow especially the work of Most 2007, and White 2002, 2006.

[4] As is well known, Hegel didn't think that the Greeks had reached the point of embodying the highest political condition fully, because they didn't fully possess the idea of the autonomous individual. Cf. Wood 1993, 200–2.

[5] In this part of the chapter, I follow Meunch 2006, Pattison 2007 and to a lesser extent Lear 2006 and Nehamas 1998.

[6] Kierkegaard focuses on Socrates in all of Part One of the dissertation and in Part Two in the second half of the chapter titled 'The World-Historical Validity of Irony, the Irony of Socrates'.

[7] *M* 341; *SVF* 14, 352.

[8] *M* 340; *SVF* 14, 350–351.

[9] Kierkegaard 1990.

[10] Kierkegaard 1990.

[11] Kierkegaard 1993; §163, 128–9.

[12] Quoted by Nehamas 1998, 128; subtitle of Nietzsche's autobiography *Ecce Homo*.

[13] Nietzsche 9.37, quoted by Nehamas 1998, 138.

[14] In this part of the chapter, I follow Porter 2000 and 2006, as well as Nehamas 1998 and Silk 2007.

[15] Quoted by Porter 2006. Porter uses the following abbreviation here: B = Friedrich Nietzsche, *Werke und Briefe. Historisch-Kritische Gesamtausgabe. Werke.* 5 vols. Ed. Hans Joachim Mette and Karl Schlechta (Munich: C. H. Beck, 1933–43).

CHAPTER NINE: CITIZEN SOCRATES

[1] Cf. Lane 2007.

[2] 'Socrates and Vietnam', in Vlastos 1994.

[3] Cf. Arendt 1990.

[4] See especially Schofield 2006.

[5] See also Villa 2000.

[6] Ryn 2005.

[7] Popper 1963. On the contrasts between Popper and Strauss see Lane 2001, and on the contrasts between Arendt and Strauss see Villa 2001.

[8] Brown, 'Socrates the Cosmopolitan', http://agora.stanford.edu/agora/libArticles/brown/brown.pdf.

CHAPTER TEN: CONCLUSION: SOCRATES AND SELF-KNOWLEDGE

[1] *Apology Charmides Theaetetus, Phaedrus, Alcibiades I* and *Euthydemus*. Of these, the *Euthydemus* exceptionally does not mention Delphi, but, as I show below, it shares the quest for what is *oikeion*, i.e. most one's own, with the *Charmides*.

[2] The story of the oracle is in this respect similar to the story of Socrates' encounter with Zopyrus: a soothsayer reports something negative about

Socrates and Socrates confirms the truth of the statement, relying on his self-knowledge for confirmation of the soothsayer's expertise.

[3] On the procedural requirement that Socrates is interested only in statements that the interlocutor holds to be true, and its relationship to the elenchus as a genuine quest for truth, see Vlastos 1991, 140: 'Since Socrates' real purpose is not merely to search out and destroy his interlocutor's conceit of knowledge, but also to advance the search for truth, if he is to find it by this method, while professing to know nothing, he must worm it out of them.' See also Benson 1992, 63–4; 2000.

[4] As Benson 1992 and Nehamas 1998 do.

[5] Irwin 1995.

[6] Brickhouse and Smith 1994.

[7] *Republic* 3369a: 'While we were speaking, Thrasymachus had tried many times to take over the discussion but was restrained by those sitting near him, who wanted to hear our argument to the end. When we paused after what I'd just said, however, he couldn't keep quiet any longer. He coiled himself up like a wild beast about to spring, and he hurled himself at us as if to tear us to pieces.'

Apology 23e4: 'Meletus being vexed on behalf of the poets, Anytus on behalf of the craftsmen and politicians.'

Meno 95a2: 'I think, Meno, that Anytus is angry, and I am not at all surprised. He thinks, to begin with, that I am slandering those men, and then believes himself to be one of them. If he ever realizes what slander is, he will cease from anger, but he does not know it now.'

[8] *Euthyphro* 6c5: 'I will, if you wish, relate many other things about the gods which I know will amaze you.'

Hippias Major 304b1: 'Here is what is fine and worth a lot; to be able to present a speech well and finely, in court or council or any other authority to whom you give the speech, to convince them and go home carrying not the smallest but the greatest of prizes, the successful defence of yourself, your property, and friends.'

[9] It is also true that in the *Hippias Major* and in the *First Alcibiades*, Socrates is interested in asking about the identity of the person. Cf. Annas 1985. Annas also shows that in the *Alcibiades I*, self-knowledge is construed as objective knowledge, as a viewpoint that is made available by stepping outside the immediacy, let us say, of one's own vantage point (129–31).

[10] Sedley 1999.

[11] Kahn 1996; Rossetti for the fragments of Phaedo's Socratic dialogues, missing from *SSR* as Kahn notes.

BIBLIOGRAPHY

All translations of Plato are taken from *Complete Works: Plato,* edited, with introduction and notes, by J. M. Cooper; associate editor, D. S. Hutchinson. Indianapolis, IN: Hackett, 1997. Occasionally the translation has been modified in order to reflect the sense of the Greek that the author wanted to bring out.

Adamson, P. 2007. 'The Arabic Socrates: The place of al-Kindi's report in the tradition', in Trapp 2007.

Adkins, A. 1960. *Merit and Responsibility.* Oxford: Clarendon Press.

Ahbel-Rappe, S. and Kamtekar, R. (eds.) 2006. *A Companion to Socrates.* London: Blackwell.

Alessi, F. 2000. *La Stoa e la tradizione Socratica.* Naples: Bibliopolis.

Alon, I. 1995. *Socrates Arabus.* Jerusalem: Hebrew University.

—. 2006. 'Arabic Socrates', in Ahbel-Rappe and Kamtekar 2006.

Annas, J. 1985. 'Self-knowledge in early Plato', in O'Meara 1985.

—. 1993. *The Morality of Happiness.* Oxford: Oxford University Press.

—. 1994. 'Plato the skeptic', in Vander Waerdt 1994.

—. 1999. *Platonic Ethics Old and New.* Ithaca, NY: Cornell University Press.

Annas, J. and Rowe, C. (eds.) 2002. *New Perspectives on Plato, Modern and Ancient.* Washington, DC: Center for Hellenic Studies.

Arendt, H. 1990. 'Philosophy and politics'. *Social Research* 57.1: 73–104.

Aristotle. 1999. *Nicomachean Ethics.* Translated with introduction, notes and glossary by T. Irwin. Indianapolis, IN: Hackett.

Ausland, H. 2002. 'Forensic characteristics of Socratic argumentation', in Scott 2002.

—. 2006. 'Socrates on definition', in Ahbel-Rappe and Kamtekar 2006.

Barney, R. 2003. 'A puzzle in Stoic ethics'. *Oxford Studies in Ancient Philosophy* 24: 303–40.

Beiser, F. (ed.) 1993. *The Cambridge Companion to Hegel*. Cambridge: Cambridge University Press.

Benson, H. (ed.) 1992. *Essays on the Philosophy of Socrates.* Oxford: Oxford University Press.

—. 2000. *Socratic Wisdom.* Oxford: Oxford University Press.

—. (ed.) 2006. *A Companion to Plato.* London: Blackwell.

Bett, R. 2002. 'Is there a Sophistic ethics?' *Ancient Philosophy* 22.2, 235–262.

—. 2006. 'Socrates and skepticism', in Ahbel-Rappe and Kamtekar 2006.

Beversluis, J. 2000. *Cross Examining Socrates*. Cambridge: Cambridge University Press.

Billot, M.-F. 1993. 'Antisthene et le Cynosarges', in Goulet-Cazé and Goulet 1993.

Blondell, R. 2002. *The Play of Character in Plato's Dialogues.* Cambridge: Cambridge University Press.

Brancacci, A. 1990. *Oikeios logos: la filosofia del linguaggio di Antistene.* Elenchos Suppl. 20. Naples: Bibliopolis.

—. 1992. 'La koinonia tra cinismo e stoicismo nel libro 6 (103–105) delle *Vite* di Diogene Laerzio'. *Aufstieg und Niedergang der römischen Welt (ANRW)* 36.6: 4049–75.

Branham, R. B. and Goulet-Cazé, M.-O. (eds.) 1996. *The Cynics: The Cynic Movement in Antiquity and Its Legacy.* Berkeley; Los Angeles, CA: University of California Press.

Brennan, T. 2005. *The Stoic Life*. Oxford: Oxford University Press.

Brickhouse, T. and Smith, N. 1994. *Plato's Socrates.* Oxford: Oxford University Press.

—. 2002. *The Trial and Execution of Socrates*. Oxford: Oxford University Press.

Brittain, C. 2006. *Cicero on Academic Scepticism*. Indianapolis, IN: Hackett.

Brown, E. 2004. 'Minding the gap in Plato's *Republic*'. *Philosophical Studies* 117.1–2: 275–302.

—. 2006, 'Socrates and the Stoa', in Ahbel-Rappe and Kamtekar 2006.

—. (Forthcoming). *Stoic Cosmopolitanism.* Cambridge: Cambridge University Press.

Burnyeat, M. 1990. *The Theaetetus of Plato*. Indianapolis, IN: Hackett.

Bussanich, J. 2006. 'Socrates and religious experience', in Ahbel-Rappe and Kamtekar 2006.

Cairns, D., Herrmann, F. and Penner, T. (eds) 2007. *Pursuing the Good: Ethics and Metaphysics in Plato's Republic*. Edinburgh: Edinburgh University Press.

Caizzi, F. D. (ed.) 1966. *Antisthenis Fragmenta*. Milan: Istituto Editoriale Cisalpino.

Clay, D. 1994. 'The origins of the Socratic dialogue', in Vander Waerdt 1994.

Cooper, J. M. 2004. *Knowledge, Nature, and the Good: Essays on Ancient Philosophy*. Princeton, NJ: Princeton University Press.

Denyer, N. (ed.) 2001. *Alcibiades/Plato*. Cambridge; New York: Cambridge University Press.

Diogenes Laertius. 1964. *Vitae philosophorvm. Recognovit breviqve adnotatione critica instrvxit H.S. Long*. Oxonii: Typographco Clarendoniano.

Dorion, L.-A. 2003. *Mémorables/Xénophon*; texte établi par M. Bandini; traduit par L.-A. Dorion. Paris: Les Belles Lettres. Budé.

—. 2006. 'Xenophon's Socrates', in Ahbel-Rappe and Kamtekar 2006.

Edwards, M. 2007. 'Socrates and the early Church', in Trapp 2007.

Fine, G. (ed.) 1999. *Plato 2*. Oxford Readings in Philosophy. Oxford: Oxford University Press.

Frischer, B. 1982. *The Sculpted Word: Epicureanism and Philosophical Recruitment in Ancient Greece*. Berkeley, CA: University of California Press.

Giannantoni, G. 1990a. *Socratis et socraticorum reliquiae (SSR)*. 4 vols. Naples: Bibliopolis.

—. 1990b. 'Antistene: la presunta fondazione della scuola cinica'. In *SSR*, 4: 223–34.

Goulbourne, R. 2007. 'Voltaire's Socrates', in Trapp 2007.

Goulet-Cazé, M.-O. 1992. 'Le Livre VI de Diogene Laerce'. *Aufstieg und Niedergang der römischen Welt (ANRW)* 36.6: 3880–4048.

—. 1996. 'Who was the first dog?' in Branham and Goulet-Cazé 1996.

Goulet-Cazé, M.-O. and Goulet, R. 1993. *Le Cynisme ancien et ses prolongements. Actes du colloque international du CNRS*, 22–25 1991. Paris: Presses Universitaires de France.

Graver, M. 2002. *Cicero on the Emotions: Tusculan Disputations 3 and 4.* Translated and with commentary by M. Graver. Chicago, IL: University of Chicago Press.

—. 2008. *The Stoics on Emotions.* Chicago, IL: University of Chicago Press.

Hegel, G. 1995. *Lectures on the History of Philosophy I: Greek Philosophy to Plato.* Trans. E. S. Haldane. London: Routledge and Kegan Paul.

Inwood, B. 1985. *Ethics and Human Action in Early Stoicism.* Oxford: Clarendon Press; New York: Oxford University Press.

Irwin, T. 1995. *Plato's Ethics.* Oxford: Oxford University Press.

Janko, R. 2002. 'The Derveni Papyrus, an interim text'. *Zeitschrift für Papyrologie und Epigraphik (ZPE)* 141: 1–62.

—. 2004. 'Review of Gabor Betegh', in *The Derveni Papyrus: Cosmology, Theology and Interpretation.* Cambridge: Cambridge University Press.

—. 2006. 'Socrates the freethinker', in Ahbel-Rappe and Kamtekar 2006.

Johnston, S. I. and Graf, F. 2007. *Ritual Texts for the Afterlife.* London; New York: Routledge.

Jowett, B. 1892. *The Dialogues of Plato*, vol. 1. Oxford: Oxford University Press (original edition 1871).

Kahn, C. H. 1996. *Plato and the Socratic Dialogue.* Cambridge: Cambridge University Press.

—. 2002. 'On Platonic chronology', in Annas and Rowe 2002.

Kamtekar, R. 1998. '*Aidos* in Epictetus'. *Classical Philology* 93: 136–60.

Kerferd, G. B. 1981. *The Sophistic Movement.* Cambridge: Cambridge University Press.

Kierkegaard, S. 1989. *The Concept of Irony with Continual Reference to Socrates (Kierkegaard's Writings*, vol. 2). Trans. H. Hong and E. Hong. Princeton, NJ: Princeton University Press (original work published 1841).

—. 1990. *For Self-Examination* and *Judge for Yourself!* Trans. H. Hong and E. Hong. Princeton, NJ: Princeton University Press.

—. 1993. *The Diary of Søren Kierkegaard.* Trans. P. Rhode. New York: Citadel Press.

—. 1998. *The Moment and Late Writings (Kierkegaard's Writings*, vol. 23). Trans. H. Hong and E. Hong. Princeton, NJ: Princeton University Press (original work published 1854–5).

King, M. L., Jr. 1986. 'Letter from Birmingham County Jail', reprinted in *A Testament of Hope: The Essential Writings of Martin Luther King.* Ed. Washington D.C. San Francisco, CA: Harper Collins.

Konstan, D. et al. 1998. On frank criticism. Atlanta: Scholars Press.

Kraut, R. 1983. 'Comments on Gregory Vlastos, "The Socratic elenchus"'. *Oxford Studies in Ancient Philosophy* 1: 59–70.

—. 1989. *Aristotle on the Human Good.* Cambridge: Cambridge University Press.

—. 1999. 'Return to the cave: *Republic* 519–521', in Fine 1999.

—. 2006. 'Socratic ethics', in Ahbel-Rappe and Kamtekar 2006.

Lane, M. 2001. *Plato's Progeny.* London: Duckworth.

—. 2007. 'Gadfly in God's own country. Socrates in 20th century America', in Trapp 2007.

Lapatin, K. 2006. 'Depicting Socrates', in Ahbel-Rappe and Kamtekar 2006.

Lear, J. 2006. 'Socrates and psychoanalysis', in Ahbel-Rappe and Kamtekar 2006.

Linck, M. 2007. *The Ideas of Socrates.* London: Continuum.

Long, A. A. 1971. *Problems in Stoicism.* London: Athlone Press.

—. 1988. 'Socrates in Hellenistic philosophy'. *Classical Quarterly* 38: 150–71.

—. 1989. 'Stoic eudaimonism'. *Proceedings of the Boston Area Colloquium in Ancient Philosophy* 4: 77–101.

—. 1996a. 'The Socratic tradition', in Branham and Goulet-Cazé 1996.

—. 1996b. *Stoic Studies.* Cambridge: Cambridge University Press.

—. 2002. *Epictetus.* Oxford: Oxford University Press.

—. 2006. *From Epicurus to Epictetus.* Oxford: Oxford University Press.

Long, A. A. and Sedley, D. 1987. *The Hellenistic Philosophers.* 2 vols. Cambridge: Cambridge University Press.

Mainz, V. 2007. 'Bringing the hemlock up: Jaques-Louis David's Socrates and the inventions of history', in Trapp 2007.

Marinoff, L. 1999. *Plato, Not Prozac!* New York: HarperCollins.

McLean, D. 2007. 'The Socratic corpus: Socrates and physiognomy' in Trapp 2007.

McPherran, M. 2003. 'Socrates, Crito, and their debt to Asclepius'. *Ancient Philosophy* 23: 71–92.

Montuori, M. 1992. *The Socratic Problem.* Amsterdam: J. C. Gieben.

Morrison, J. 1994. 'Xenophon's Socrates as teacher', in Vander Waerdt 1994.

Most, G. 1993. 'A cock for Asclepius'. *Classical Quarterly* 43: 96–111.

—. 2007. 'Socrates in Hegel', in Trapp 2007.

Muench, P. 2006. 'Kierkegaard's Socratic point of view', in Ahbel-Rappe and Kamtekar 2006.

Nails, D. 2000. 'Mouthpiece, smouthpiece', in Press 2000.

—. 2002. *The People of Plato*. Indianapolis, IN: Hackett.

—. 2006. 'The trial and death of Socrates', in Ahbel-Rappe and Kamtekar 2006.

Nehamas, A. 1998. *The Art of Living.* Berkeley; Los Angeles, CA: University of California Press.

—. 1998. *Virtues of Authenticity*. Princeton, NJ: Princeton University Press.

Nehamas, A. and Woodruff, P. 1997. *Plato: Complete Works.* Ed. J. Cooper. Indianapolis, IN: Hackett.

Nietzsche, F. 1994. *On the Genealogy of Morals*. Trans. C. Diethe. Cambridge: Cambridge University Press.

—. 1999. *The Birth of Tragedy*. Cambridge Texts in the History of Philosophy. Cambridge: Cambridge University Press.

Nussbaum M. 1980. 'Aristophanes and Socrates on learning practical wisdom'. *Yale Classical Studies* 26: 43–97.

O'Connor, D. 1994. 'The erotic self-sufficiency of Socrates', in Vander Waerdt 1994.

O'Meara, D. (ed.) 1985. *Platonic Investigations*. Washington, DC: Catholic University of America.

—. 1989. *Pythagoras Revived*. Oxford: Oxford University Press.

—. 2003. *Platonopolis*. Oxford: Oxford University Press.

Pangle, T. 1994. 'Socrates in the context of Xenophon's political writings', in Vander Waerdt 1994.

Pattison, G. 2007. 'A simple wise man of olden times', in Trapp 2007.

Pendrick, G. J. 2002. *Antiphon the Sophist. The Fragments*. Edited with introduction, translation and commentary by G. J. Pendrick. Cambridge: Cambridge University Press.

Penner, T. 2007a. 'The good, advantage, happiness and the form of the good: How continuous with Socratic ethics is Platonic ethics?' in Cairns, Herrmann and Penner 2007.

—. 2007b. 'What is the form of the good the form of? A question about the plot of the *Republic*', in Cairns, Herrmann and Penner 2007.

Penner, T. and Rowe, C. 2005. *Plato's Lysis*. Cambridge: Cambridge University Press.

Phillips, C. 2001. *Socrates Café*. New York: Norton.

Popper, K. R. 1963. *The Open Society and Its Enemies*. 4th edn rev. Princeton, NJ: Princeton University Press.

Porter, J. 2000. *The Invention of Dionysus: An Essay on the Birth of Tragedy*. Palo Alto, CA: Stanford University Press

——. 2006. 'Nietzsche and "The problem of Socrates"', in Ahbel-Rappe and Kamtekar 2006.

Press, G. (ed.) 2000. *Who Speaks for Plato?* Lanham, MD: Rowman & Littlefield

Prince, S. H. 1997. 'Antisthenes on language, thought, and culture'. Ph.D. diss., University of Michigan.

——. 2006. 'Socrates, Antisthenes and the Cynics', in Ahbel-Rappe and Kamtekar 2006.

Pucci, P. 2002. *Xenophon. Socrates' Defense*. Supplementi di Lexis 10 Amsterdam: Hakkert.

Rankin, H. D. 1983. *Sophists, Socratics, and Cynics*. London: Barnes and Noble.

Rappe, S. 2000. 'Father of the dogs? Cynic elements in Plato's *Euthydemus*'. *Classical Philology* 95: 281–302.

Reshotko, N. (ed.) 2004. *Plato and Socrates: Desire, Identity, and Existence*. Kelowna, BC: Academic Printing Press.

——. 2006. *Socratic Virtue: Making the Best of the Neither-Good-Nor-Bad*. Cambridge: Cambridge University Press.

Riley, M. 1980. 'The Epicurean criticism of Socrates'. *Phoenix* 34, 55–68.

Ross, D. 1924. *Aristotle's Metaphysics. A Revised Text with Introduction and Commentary*. Oxford: Clarendon Press.

Rossetti, L. 1980. 'Richerche sui "dialoghi socratici" di Fedone e di Euclide'. *Hermes* 108.

Rowe, C. 2006. 'Socrates in Plato's dialogues', in Ahbel-Rappe and Kamtekar 2006.

——. 2007a. 'The form of the good and the good in Plato's *Republic*', in Cairns, Herrmann and Penner 2007.

——. 2007b. *Plato and the Art of Philosophical Writing*. Cambridge: Cambridge University Press.

Rudebusch, G. 2004. 'Socratic Perfectionism', in Reshotko 2004.

——. 2006. 'Socratic Eros', in Ahbel-Rappe and Kamtekar 2006.

—. 2007. 'Neutralism in book I of the *Republic*', in Cairns, Herrmann and Penner 2007.

Ryn, C. G. 2005. *Humanitas* 54.18.1–2.

Schleiermacher, F. 1818. 'Über den Werth des Sokrates als Philosophen' (On the Value of Socrates as a Philosopher). Trans. C. Thirwall, reprinted in Xenophon's *Memorabilia of Socrates* (1883). Ed. C. Anthon. New York: Harper Bros, 442–8.

Schmid, W. T. 1998. *Plato's Charmides and the Socratic Ideal of Rationality*. Albany, NY: SUNY Press.

Schofield. 2006. *Founders of Modern Thought. Plato*. Oxford: Oxford University Press.

Scott, G. (ed.) 2002. *Does Socrates Have a Method?* University Park, PA: Penn State Press.

Sedley, D. 1999. 'The ideal of godlikeness', in Fine 2002.

—. 2004. *The Midwife of Platonism*. Oxford: Oxford University Press.

—. 2008. *Creationism and Its Critics in Antiquity*. Berkeley; Los Angeles, CA: University of California Press.

Silk, M. 2007. 'Nietzsche's Socrateases', in Trapp 2007.

Silk, M. and Stern, J. P. 1981. *Nietzsche on Tragedy*. Cambridge: Cambridge University Press.

Smith, N. D. and Woodruff, P. (eds.) 2000. *Reason and Religion in Socratic Philosophy*. Oxford: Oxford University Press.

Sorabji, R. 2000. *Emotion and Peace of Mind: From Stoic Agitation to Christian Temptation*. Oxford; New York: Oxford University Press.

—. 2006. *Self: Ancient and Modern Insights*. Oxford: Oxford University Press.

Sprague, R. K. 1962. *Plato's Use of Fallacy*. New York: Routledge and Kegan Paul.

Steiner, G. 1996. 'Two suppers', in *No Passion Spent: Essays 1978–1996*. New Haven, CT; London: Yale University Press.

Stevens, J. 1994. 'Friendship and profit in Xenophon's *Oeconomicus*', in Vander Waerdt 2004.

Stone, I. F. 1989. *The Trial of Socrates*. New York: Anchor Books.

Strauss, L. 1964. *The City and the Man*. Chicago, IL: University of Chicago Press.

—. 1970. *Xenophon's Socratic Discourse*. Ithaca, NY: Cornell University Press.

Striker, G. 1994. 'Plato's Socrates and the Stoics', in Vander Waerdt 1994.

—. 1996. *Essays on Hellenistic Philosophy and Ethics.* Cambridge: Cambridge University Press.

Tarrant, H. 2002. 'Elenchos and exetasis: Capturing the purpose of Socratic interrogation', in Scott 2002.

—. 2006. 'Socratic method and Socratic truth', in Ahbel-Rappe and Kamtekar 2006.

Teichmüller, G. 1881. *Literarische Fehden im vierten Jahrhundert vor Christus* Breslau: W. Koebner.

Trapp, M. (ed.) 2007. *Socrates in the Nineteenth and Twentieth Centuries.* London: Ashgate.

Tsouna-McKirahan, V. 1998. *The Epistemology of the Cyrenaic School.* Cambridge; New York: Cambridge University Press.

Tuplin, C. (ed.) 1999. *Xenophon and His World.* Stuttgart: Fran Steiner.

Vander Waerdt, P. 1993. 'Socratic justice and self-sufficiency'. *Oxford Studies in Ancient Philosophy* 11: 1–43.

—. (ed.) 1994. *The Socratic Movement.* Berkeley; Los Angeles, CA: University of California Press.

Villa, D. (ed.) 2000. *The Cambridge Companion to Hannah Arendt.* Cambridge: Cambridge University Press.

—. 2001. *Socratic Citizenship.* Princeton, NJ: Princeton University Press.

Vlastos, G. 1973. *Platonic Studies.* Princeton, NJ: Princeton University Press.

—. 1983. 'The Socratic elenchus'. *Oxford Studies in Ancient Philosophy* 1: 27–58.

—. 1985. 'Socrates' disavowal of knowledge'. *Classical Quarterly* 35: 1–31.

—. 1988. 'Elenchus and mathematics. A turning-point in Plato's philosophical development'. *American Journal of Philology* 109: 362–96.

—. 1991. *Socrates, Ironist and Moral Philosopher.* Ithaca, NY: Cornell University Press.

—. 1994. *Socratic Studies.* Ed. M. Burnyeat. Oxford: Oxford University Press.

Vogt, K. 2008. *Law, Reason, and the Cosmic City.* Oxford: Oxford University Press.

Waterfield, R. 1999. 'Xenophon's Socratic mission', in Tuplin 1999.

Weiss, R. 2006. *The Socratic Paradox and Its Enemies.* Chicago, IL: University of Chicago Press.

White, N. 2002. *Individual and Conflict in Greek Ethics*. Oxford: Oxford University Press.

—. 2006. 'Socrates in Hegel', in Ahbel-Rappe and Kamtekar 2006.

White, S. 1995. 'Thrasymachus the diplomat'. *Classical Philology* 90.4: 307–27.

—. 2000. 'Socrates and his daimonion', in Smith and Woodruff 2000.

Wilson, E. 2007. *The Death of Socrates*. Princeton, NJ Princeton University Press.

Wood, A. 1993. 'Hegel's ethics', in Beiser 1993.

Woodruff, P. 2006. 'Socrates among the Sophists', in Ahbel-Rappe and Kamtekar 2006.

Woolf, R. 2000. 'Callicles and Socrates'. *Oxford Studies in Ancient Philosophy* 18: 1–40.

INDEX OF PASSAGES

GENERAL INDEX

Charmides 50, 53, 75
  on temperance 107
choice (*prohairesis*) 103
Christianity
  Kierkegaard on 119–20
chronology of dialgoues 52
Cicero
  Academica 11, 105, 106
  on good life 95
civic discourse 144
civil disobedience 2, 127–36
  of *Apology* 130, 131
  Socratic 129
civil rights movement 129, 132
classical philology,
        nineteenth-century 2
complicity and passivity 129
complicity in laws, *Crito* 130
condemnation to death of
        Socrates 17
effect on Plato 136
conscience, voice of 126
Continental philosophers,
        20th century 127
contradictions 54
corruption of youth,
        accusation 19
courage 50, 55–6, 65–7, 70–1
  in death 8
  definition 80
  manly virtue (*andreia*) 98
craft-model for virtue 72
Crates, founder of Stoa 96
Critias 22
Crito 52, 127–9, 133
  on injustice 92
Cynics 8, 10, 11, 95–9
Cyrus the younger 42

Daimonion, of Nietzsche 124
David, Jacques Louis, death of
        Socrates, painting 30

death of Socrates 15
  meaning in history 28–31
  those present 4
death penalty vote by jury 21
'decree of Diopeithes' 24
definition
  of moral terms 70
  in Socratic dialogues 71
deliberation 118
Delphic Oracle 66
  in *Apology* 144–6
  consulting the 42
democracy, Socrates' attitude
        to 133
Derveni Papyrus 26
desire arousal, lesson in 45–6
desires
  disowning of
        conventional 149
  domination of 60
  good or not good 101, 149
developmentalism 48–52
Diagoras of Melos, crime
        of 25–6
dialogues of definition 66, 70
Diderot, Denis, translation of
        Plato's *Apology* 30
diminishment of
        interlocutor 56–7
Diogenes Laertius 27, 37
  on Anaxagoras' prosecution
        for impiety 25
  on good and bad 100
  Life of Antisthenes 97
  *Lives of the Eminent
        Philosophers* 4, 10, 96
Diogenes of Apollonia 26
Diogenes of Sinope, as dog 98
Dionysus and Apollo 125
disagreement of witnesses 9
disobedience to law 129
Dissoi Logoi, treatise 35, 71, 72

temperance 70, 71, 75, 151
 definition 80
 as virtue (*Charmides*) 55, 90
Theaetetus and Socratic
  midwifery 152–4
theology of Diagoras 26
Theseus in labyrinth 53
Think-o-mat 9, 25, 33, 34
Thirty
 refusal to cooperate 132
 rule of, in Athens 18, 21–2
Thrasymachus (*Republic* I) 35,
  71, 93
totalitarian regimes 127, 140, 141
traditional values 35
Tragedy and Dialectic 125
tragic of Hegel's Socrates 15–21,
  116
trial and imprisonment of
  Socrates 127–9
 and of Jesus 136
true witness bearing 36
truth
 for own sake 139
 happiness and 82
 knowledge of 61
 multiple perspectives 71
 remedy for ignorance 109
 service of 112

Unitarian reading of Plato 48,
  49
unity of virtues 111
universal definition 3
utopian state 140

vice and virtue 101
Vietnam war, protesters
  against 132
vindication of Socrates 46
virtue (arête) 11, 36, 43, 51,
  75–6, 87
 benefit to person 90

definition 73, 98
ignorance of 40
importance of 112
as knowledge 64, 73, 92,
  108
promotion of 145–6
as self-knowledge 146–52
and Socratic ethics 86
teaching of 68–9, 72, 73, 76
as wisdom 88, 147
virtue-centred
  eudaimonism 147
virtue ethics 43–4
Vlastos, Gregory 49–52, 57
 on *Apology* 135
 on elenctic refutation 75–8
 on Plato and Socrates 6
 Socratic Elenchus 73
Voltaire, *Dictionnaire
  philosophique* 30
Vortex, worship of 46

weakness of will 105
wealth or poverty in souls 38
well-being, desire for 91
wisdom 58, 59, 139, 151
 desire for 45
 as good 82, 99, 100
 or ignorance 59
 of Socrates 144
 teaching of 72
words
 in *Euthyphro* 69
 in *Laches* 69
writings
 of Socrates, none 6
 of Socratics 32
wrongdoing 90–2

Xanthippe, wife of Socrates
  1, 17
Xenophon 2, 3, 38
 on Socrates 43